An

Angelwalk

Novel

ON HOLY GROUND

An

ROGER
Angelwalk
ELWOOD
Novel

In association with Southwestern Baptist Theological Seminary

Appreciation is expressed to Steeple Hill Books for their permission to allow Roger Elwood to take time off from his *Angelwalk* series for Steeple Hill to do this very special entry into the *Angelwalk* franchise. It is a one-time only exception, for which we are grateful, and we wish them the best with their own books.

ON HOLY GROUND

F
ELW

Destiny Image Fiction

An imprint of

Destiny Image® Publishers, Inc.
P.O. Box 310
Shippensburg, PA 17257-0310

ISBN 0-7684-2114-4

For Worldwide Distribution
Printed in the U.S.A.

This book and all other Destiny Image, Revival Press, MercyPlace, Fresh Bread, Destiny Image Fiction, and Treasure House books are available at Christian bookstores and distributors worldwide.

For a U.S. bookstore nearest you, call **1-800-722-6774**.
For more information on foreign distributors, call **717-532-3040**.
Or reach us on the Internet: **www.reapernet.com**

iv

Dedicated to

Sydney, Shawn

and Kim

—for now, for eternity

To have faith is one thing; to have faith in the midst of the most tragic circumstances is quite another.

Anonymous

Acknowledgments

Let me thank, from the center of my soul, Dorothy Elwood, my dear struggling, grieving mother, and, posthumously, Raymond Elwood, my father, for being so crucial to my life for so long—nearly 57 years, a lifetime in itself perhaps—which is what has made my father's death so shattering.

I also want to thank Dr. John Babler, who has encouraged me personally through the darkest moments of demonic oppression as I was writing this book.

I should note that the royalties from this book will be used to fund scholarships and cash grants as well as much needed computer and related equipment, in memory of Sydney Browning, Shawn Brown and Kim Jones at Southwestern Baptitst Theological Seminary (SWBTS).

An office from which to direct the distribution of funds will be set up at one of the colleges or universities—though not at SWBTS—in order to ensure an impartial selection of recipients. SWBTS was important to Sydney, Shawn and Kim, but they also anticipated forming or joining ministries apart from SWBTS; thus it seems their memories would be best served by broadening the outreach of the revenue from the book that you, the reader, are holding now.

All disbursements as scholarships, plus limited expenses and such, will be properly delineated.

I count all that part of my life lost which I spent not in communion with God, or in doing good.

John Donne

Contents

Introduction 1
Author's Note 9
Foreword 15
Prologue #1 23
Prologue #2 29

Part I **33**
Chapter 1 35
Chapter 2 39
Chapter 3 43
Chapter 4 47
Chapter 5 53
Chapter 6 57
Chapter 7 63
Chapter 8 67
Chapter 9 71

Part II **75**
Chapter 10 77
Chapter 11 81
Chapter 12 85

Chapter 13 91
Chapter 14 95

Part III **99**
Chapter 15 101
Chapter 16 105
Epilogue 109

Afterword **113**
"Where Was God?" (Kenneth Hemphill) 115

Appendix **137**
"The Devil Was Doing a Dance in God's Playground"
            (Dr. Ian Jones) 139

Author's Confession 143

The urge toward violence is part of human nature, the part influenced by the prince of darkness...master of evil...the leader of all other fallen angels.

Alfred Wayne Abbott

Introduction

Introduction

February 14, 2000.

Soon after I arrived here in Fort Worth, Texas, on that date, my purpose being to live and work on the sprawling and well-kept 200-acre campus of nearly a century-old Southwestern Baptist Theological Seminary, I was to find that my initial assignment from president Kenneth Hemphill happened to be the book, as I have titled it, *Angelwalk*: ON HOLY GROUND.

This was a task certain to carry with it some not inconsiderable emotional baggage, including the preceding traumas of the author as delineated in the Acknowledgments section, and, it would seem, a case of poor timing.

You see, I almost invariably become emotionally and spiritually "involved" in the various books I write, feeling each scene as though I was a part of it myself. I knew how "heavy" this book would be with its inherent tragedy, a shocker even in an age where sudden awful events explode almost regularly across our attention through media coverage and the like.

I was not sure that I could handle the additional stress; at the same time, the potential of a fresh "take" and of new insights challenged me. In the end, I was happy to accept, pledging my best efforts to do a book that undoubtedly would have substantial impact on each and every reader.

I knew that President Hemphill had the right instincts when he asked that I concentrate on the three SWBTS martyrs. More had been written about their murderer than about Kim, Sydney and Shawn combined—the attraction of evil transcendent apparently, a fascination with it evident in media around the world.

This ratio had to be changed as a matter of real honor, and the book dedicated to certain truths.

Truths.

An ancient writer penned, "What we have in us of the image of God is the love of truth and justice."

That was what I felt compelled to do: present the truly pertinent truths while writing *Angelwalk*: ON HOLY GROUND, without such meaningless details as what they had to eat the day they died, what music they listened to, what phone calls they made—without a myriad of largely insignificant details, many dragged in from front field, as the expression goes, just to seem comprehensive.

Depth and truth.

Of course!

What subject demands these twin elements more than the Wedgwood tragedy and its offshoot considerations?

Which is precisely what the president of Southwestern Baptist Theological Seminary was after...and, yes, something else.

Emotion.

This was the third part of the foundation upon which Ken Hemphill earnestly wanted me to "build" the book, joining truth and the emphasis on SWBTS and its three martyrs.

He asked me to incorporate emotion as well, rather than bury it under a mountain of minutia—a wish echoed by Stephanie Jones, the mother of Kim Jones, one of the seven victims and a student at SWBTS.

But there is truly more, a great deal more, to the story at hand than even this: What were the lives of these three outstanding young people like before they were rushed from this world?

We know, of course, that all three had been truly energetic Southwestern Baptist Theological Seminary students, studying hard in order that they might be properly trained to go unto all the world and spread the Good News, as Christ had directed.

To celebrate life in the midst of a story about bone-chilling tragedy is difficult to portray but wholly necessary in order to understand what has enabled family members and friends to get past the pain.

This I have tried earnestly to do but not at all coldly, dispassionately, with a near-clinical detachment, since the latter would have been tantamount to making this book seem like little more than an elongated news bulletin, and there had been too much of that sort of thing already.

Hundreds of pages of facts are barren, Mrs. Jones felt, if emotions are buried under them, which was my very objection to much of what had seen print about the Wedgwood shootings.

Facts edify and enlighten—no doubt about that—but it is emotions that, in the end, motivate, that hopefully force people into action, action that becomes a kind of purgative for their emotions.

Motivate...

This is certainly an important raison d'etre for *Angelwalk*: ON HOLY GROUND—perhaps the only reason for being that it has frankly, apart from what Dr. Hemphill wants to accomplish.

To motivate readers.

That is the central thread, the central thread that holds *Angelwalk*: ON HOLY GROUND together, which is, frankly, a book that may well prove to be exceedingly traumatic to read if you happened to have been a participant in and observer of the tragedy that hit Wedgwood Baptist Church so starkly, or, perhaps, a family member who came to learn about the nightmare after it had happened, your own personal nightmare only beginning at that point.

My quest was for details showing what the three martyrs were like, each one a vibrant young Christian, to be sure, as well as the nature of their lives as students at SWBTS: how they were regarded on campus by faculty members and other students alike, particularly friends who were sufficiently through the grieving process to be able to talk on the record.

I also have sought earnestly to tell the stories of Sydney Browning, Kim Jones and Shawn Brown in what might correctly be called a rather unique framework, very much comparable to the specialized approach of my *Angelwalk* series but emphasizing the factual instead.

Fortunately, once I started to head in that direction, my current *Angelwalk* publisher, Steeple Hill, kindly consented to let me borrow some of the continuing story elements from those books for *Angelwalk*: ON HOLY GROUND, making it an amalgamation of two genres, hopefully strengthening both.

You see, I was not even marginally interested in simply copying some part of what had been written before, and copiously so, especially a book by a respected SWBTS colleague, Dan Crawford.

Surprisingly, the worldwide secular media were unusually respectful in what and how they reported the Wedgwood story, its ingredients appealing apparently to their finer instincts.

Instead of trying to demean Christians and their faith, as was typical in the past, the media seemed mightily impressed by the aftermath, that is, Christians getting together in mourning as could be expected but also giving forth with praise, honor and glory to the King of Kings, not in a manner that seemed "put on" but which came from the center of their souls.

What I present to you all as readers now hopefully represents a fresh kind of journalism, one of which Warren Wiersbe wrote, "I hope the book...[will]...heal many broken hearts and lead many to the Savior."

This journalism is wrapped with love and respect in a framework of the angelic, which seems more than appropriate given the circumstances of what happened, a framework that presents facts with a wholly new dimension and fresh insights merged with a fictional overlay.

May you, the reader, be edified...that is my hope, my prayer.

I think of the young whom God has called to Himself as away at school…at the best school in the universe, under the best teachers, learning the best things, in the best manner possible.

Bishop Jacques Bossuet

Author's Note

Author's Note

I have attempted a multi-layered book that deals separately with areas that are interconnected…interconnected in terms of how spiritual warfare and the supernatural impact the world we actually see around us.

…*the world we see around us.*

For example: facts about the three SWBTS martyrs.

These are important so that the reader has some idea of what they were like, the tragedy and the triumph becoming even more powerful, rather than just statistics in a newspaper or magazine.

But there is another factor that directly impacts what happened to them that evening at Wedgwood Baptist Church.

…*spiritual warfare.*

The undeniable reality of the supernatural dimension that does exist beyond our normal sight.

Supernatural/spiritual warfare is the one element given blatantly short shrift, if it is mentioned at all, by media coverage about what happened at Wedgwood Baptist Church that night of madness.

But if the supernatural/demonic is ignored, then true relief may not be possible for those who have never benefited from Scripture-based counseling. And why pretend that this dimension to life does not exist, or carry an outlook that comes close to saying the same thing?

Many Christian counselors have fallen prey to a near-humanistic view of life and death, though they may not be aware that they are serving the purposes of satan by espousing it.

Even men of integrity seem deluded by a greater emphasis on the psychological rather than the spiritual/supernatural.

One of the most crucial elements in *Angelwalk*: ON HOLY GROUND, this suggests the greatest controversy of all, a tug-of-war between modern psychology and ancient biblical wisdom.

Christian counselors who do not make use of the supernatural knowledge that is available to them through the Bible are forsaking the greatest source of healing that exists today.

...the flesh wars against the spirit, and the spirit against the flesh.

A persistent theme indeed from Genesis through Revelation.

And one that C. S. Lewis handled so very well in his classic works, *The Screwtape Letters*.

Indeed, it is to Lewis that I dedicate these portions of *Angelwalk*: ON HOLY GROUND.

Roger Elwood
Southwestern Baptist Theological Seminary
Fort Worth, Texas

Courage is a theory until it is tried in a crucible of real tumult.

William Colbert

Foreword

Foreword

On September 15, 1999, I was looking forward to several days of study at the church I attend in Fort Worth, Texas. John MacArthur was teaching a Shepherds Conference and I had been able to clear my schedule so I could attend.

At the end of Dr. MacArthur's teaching that night, we were told that a shooting had occurred at a sister church in town. That church was Wedgwood Baptist Church and the shooting came to be the context for this book.

I immediately went to Wedgwood just a few miles away and found a thoroughly chaotic scene at the elementary school across the street from the church. News helicopters were flying over-head, parked cars lined the residential streets surrounding the church, emergency service personnel were everywhere, and there were numerous people milling around the school.

One large group of people included those who had been at the church when the shooting occurred, and they were quickly taken to a nearby police station so that officers could take their statements.

Many of those who had come to help minister or counsel went with this group to provide support. Several of us stayed at the school to support those who were left. As the hours unfolded, the realization began to set in for those left in the school that their loved ones were most likely dead.

At about 2:30 Thursday morning, the medical examiner began the process of formally notifying the family members of those who had died. During each notification, a counselor and minister accompanied the medical examiner to provide support for the family members.

As I was participating in this process, the reality of the tragedy began to sink in with great intimacy.

During the long hours of waiting and the time of the forthcoming death notifications, I observed a "peace that passes understanding" among those family members who were present along with hope and faith in the Living, Loving God of the universe. Hope/faith were present.

A little later Thursday morning, I went to Brewer High School in White Settlement, a suburb of Fort Worth. A group of 18 from First Baptist Church of White Settlement had been at Wedgwood the night before.

One of the young people from that group was killed at Wedgwood; another was wounded. These youth attended Brewer and the school invited local ministers to come and provide counseling and support to the students. It was during the time at the school that I caught a glimpse of the beginning of God's plan to bring good out of the tragedy at Wedgwood.

The Bible tells of a "family secret" for those who are in the family of God. Romans 8:28-29 (NAS) states, "And **we know** that God causes all things to work together for good to those who love God, to those who are called according to His purpose. For those whom He foreknew, He also predestined to become conformed to the image of His Son, so that He would be the firstborn among many brethren." Christians know that God brings good out of evil.

Thursday morning September 16, 1999, at Brewer High School, many hurting students encountered the love of Christ and the good news of Christianity in the midst of a tragedy.

Many of them recognized that they (like all of us) can not meet God's standards. They humbly turned away from their sins, sought God's forgiveness through Christ, and committed to follow Him.

The good that God brought out of the tragedy for these students will impact them not only for the rest of their lives here on earth, but also for eternity as they can now count on spending it in Heaven with Jesus.

A little later on that Thursday morning, many of the students from Brewer began walking over to First Baptist Church. The pastor and staff at the church were very gracious and allowed me the opportunity to serve with them during the intense days following the shooting.

Many people from the community came to the church seeking answers, and the Good News of Jesus was shared with them. Many were already committed to Christ and the Church as a body supported and encouraged each other. It was in working with this church that I began to see another application of the verses just cited as God conformed His people to the image of Christ in a miraculous way.

As I reflect back on my own involvement in the aftermath of the Wedgwood shooting, several things stand out. The first is mentioned above, namely, that the God of the universe really is in the business of bringing ultimate good out of evil for those who love Him.

I reflect back on the biblical stories of Joseph and Job and others, and I find great comfort in the fact that God is in control and brings good out of the worst tragedies. Two other things that stand out in my memory are emotional and spiritual aspects of the tragedy.

The first people I had a chance to minister to on the night of the shooting were a Fort Worth fireman and his daughter. He had been working that night and was a first responder to the scene.

His daughter was attending the rally at Wedgwood.

After not finding her outside the church, he went inside and looked at all the bodies to see if his daughter was one of them. She was not, and they were soon reunited, but it is hard to imagine the emotions that would have accompanied this father looking for his daughter in this situation. This is one of countless examples of the intense emotions that were prevalent in the midst of the crisis.

The spiritual aspects of the tragedy include that which was mentioned earlier, but go beyond it, too. The Bible teaches that there is an ongoing cosmic battle between the Kingdom of Light and the Kingdom of Darkness. "For our struggle is not against flesh and blood, but against the rulers, against the powers, against the world forces of this darkness, against the spiritual forces of wickedness in the heavenly places" (Eph. 6:12 NAS). The Wedgwood crisis happened in the midst of this struggle.

The book you hold in your hand is an attempt by my colleague as well as brother-in-Christ, Roger Elwood, to cause you to think about the Wedgwood crisis in light of this battle.

He has researched the facts around the Wedgwood tragedy and presents them faithfully. He also does a fine job of bringing out the intense emotional struggles of some of those affected by the shooting.

The unique contribution of *Angelwalk*: ON HOLY GROUND lies, however, in the introduction of characters from the spiritual realm.

The Bible teaches the existence of both angels and demons, but we are given few details about their day-to-day operations in the midst of the struggle referenced above. Roger provides us with a possible picture of how this spiritual realm might have impacted Wedgwood.

It is my prayer that, after you finish reading this strikingly unique book, you will be driven by it to the Word of God.

Although the book provides us with a possible picture of the workings of the spiritual realm, God's "divine power has granted us everything pertaining to life and godliness, through the true knowledge of Him who called us by His own glory and excellence" (2 Pet. 1:3 NAS).

Part of the good that God wants to bring out of the Wedgwood tragedy is for you to become more knowledgeable of Him, more like Him, and better equipped to minister to those around you.

The Bible is able to teach us, train us in righteousness, and equip us for every good work (see 2 Tim. 3:16-17), so it should be the vehicle through which God brings this about in your life.

In regard to spiritual warfare, the Bible teaches us that while satan is a powerful foe, God has given us what we need to stand strong against him. I leave you with these verses and a challenge to prayerfully apply them to your life:

Submit therefore to God. Resist the devil and he will flee from you (James 4:7 NAS).

Be of sober spirit, be on the alert. Your adversary, the devil, prowls around like a roaring lion, seeking someone to devour. But resist him, firm in your faith, knowing that the same experiences of suffering are being accomplished by your brethren who are in the world (1 Peter 5:8-9 NAS).

Finally, be strong in the Lord, and in the strength of His might. Put on the full armor of God, so that you will be able to stand firm against the schemes of the devil. For our struggle is not against flesh and blood, but against the rulers, against the powers, against the world forces of this darkness, against the spiritual forces of wickedness in the heavenly places. Therefore, take up the full armor of God, that you will be able to resist in the evil day, and having done everything, to stand firm. Stand firm therefore, having girded your loins with truth, and having put on the breastplate of righteousness, and having shod your feet with the preparation of the gospel of peace; in addition to all, taking up the shield of faith with which you will be able to extinguish all the flaming arrows of the evil one. And take the helmet of salvation, and the sword of the Spirit, which is the word of God (Ephesians 6:10-17 NAS).

John Babler
Department of Social Work and Ministry-Based Evangelism
Southwestern Baptist Theological Seminary

Prologue #1

What is a martyr? It is someone who dies for their faith, whether they realize that they are in the firing line or not. Perhaps they would not have been there in the first place if it had not been for that very faith.

Roger Elwood

Prologue #1

Only God could tell the future.

It was one of several abilities that had been denied satan, which further enraged the fallen prince of darkness.

Scripture proved very clear about that.

Which was why any and all astrologers, fortune-tellers, tree-leaf readers, numerologists and the like were either frauds or demonically controlled puppets, trying to deceive if possible the very elect.

An angel named Darien was especially disturbed by those who called themselves psychics.

"How dishonest they are!" he exclaimed. "They work with fallen angels posing as deceased loved ones."

"I wonder how many realize the identity of the forces that they are tapping into when they do this," remarked Stedfast, also an angel, one who had had a legendary journey named Angelwalk during which he uncovered the reasons why satan and the other fallen creatures truly deserved their ultimate punishment forever and ever in the lake of fire.

They had just encountered a situation where tragedy had struck, and an enterprising psychic, reading the obituary section of a local newspaper, contacted the bereaved family.

After presenting himself and what he could "do" for the survivors, he was turned down.

But, undeterred, he went ahead and tried another potentially lucrative would-be client.

The same reaction.

Yet this deluded individual would not be stopped. Finally, on the third try, this psychic hit pay dirt.

"Leeches!" Stedfast exclaimed.

"The worst kind," agreed Darien.

As they recalled these moments, and how they had stepped in and revealed the truth to the grieving family by showing the true character of those demons posing as their loved one, the two angels were waiting in Heaven for their next assignment and engaging in an angelic equivalent of shooting-the-breeze.

Such instances of idleness were quite rare, for though there were tens of thousands of angels throughout creation, that figure came right up against hundreds of millions of human beings who, at any given moment, would need their attention in one way or another.

"I will be glad when all of this is over," Stedfast spoke, wings fluttering as he considered the centuries, centuries of tragedy—masses of men, women and children dying on battlefields from country to country; or as the victims of epidemics; but especially perhaps the largest group of all, those babies dying at the hands of deluded doctors and nurses through the unholy and maniacal practice of abortion, a practice of the most grotesque barbarism.

"So frightened," Darien recalled. "Their cries of pain! Poor helpless little ones! That there is even a debate astounds me."

"The low level of human morality!"

Both had welcomed the souls of vast numbers of infants into Heaven, infants with new bodies no longer missing arms or legs, no longer with their skulls split open, no longer poisoned by saline solution as they gasped for air, confused and panicked and terrified by what it was that was happening to them after months of warmth and security of the darkness of their mother's womb.

"How can it not be murder?" Stedfast asked.

"Because of delusion," the other angel reminded him. "But there is a time when the perpetrators shall see the truth, when they themselves

are going to be at the point of death, and, therefore, no longer able to bury their corrupted consciences under layers of expediency."

"And, suddenly, all the pain of the helpless children they have slaughtered is visited upon them."

Stedfast was not gloating but feeling genuine sorrow for murderers and victims alike.

"If only they had listened," he groaned, "if only they had allowed themselves to see—"

He was interrupted by a command, a summons from God Himself, Darien and he now being given their latest assignment.

To go to Texas.

To a respected nearly century-old seminary in Fort Worth.

And then to a church just a few miles away.

"What are we to do when we arrive there, Father?" both angels asked rather tremulously of their blessed heavenly Creator. "What is our purpose to be in each of these places?"

God told them.

"Three murdered from just the seminary alone...?" Darien asked, barely able to communicate as his heavenly Father gave him a vision of what was to ensue, and to Stedfast as well.

Both had learned not to question but to accept His wisdom, and so neither objected.

"When, dear Father?" Stedfast inquired with some anxiety. "When shall we do this?"

God said that they were to go immediately.

So the two angels quickly walked the path between Heaven and earth, a path with a special name.

Angelwalk.

And Darien as well as Stedfast descended, though reluctantly by virtue of the nature of their assignment, immediately after they left the presence of their Creator for whom they felt love eternal.

First stop: Southwestern Baptist Theological Seminary.

Prologue #2

Courage in danger is half the battle.
Plautus

Prologue #2

Darien and Stedfast intended Southwestern Baptist Theological Seminary to be the first stop, but their Creator had other plans.

Columbine High.

They visited that school, and listened to what teachers and students were still discussing so many months later. A tragedy so horrendous would hang on psychologically for a long time. Shaking it from themselves was not a cut-and-dried task.

"So much pain..." Stedfast said.

"Inflicted by satan working through puppets," Darien added. "We have seen it before, but each time the enormity hits us as hard as a physical blow would to a human being."

By their peers.

Confused, enraged young men spewing forth their poison.

And left behind as their debilitating legacy was the anguish of the wounded, those who were bodily wounded, alongside those who had perhaps the worst wounds of all, to their minds, their hearts—their every stability as functional adults at stake as the weeks, months and years passed.

One could no longer stand it and hung himself in his bedroom.

Another, a mother, purchased a gun and shot herself to death in front of the startled salesperson.

"Evil comes in and takes control by stages," Darien spoke, "with individuals and—"

"That applies to organizations, Christian as well as secular," Stedfast interjected. "They can be in existence for a long time and seemingly unassailable, and yet something happens."

If Darien had been of flesh and blood, he would have sighed in despair and resignation.

"Acts of violence capture the most attention," he pointed out, "but satan can be more insidious than that, his scheme like hidden cancer eating away at the spiritual vitality of a church or some other institution."

As they went their way, they remembered the other shootings at other schools and saw the link between the degradation of certain institutions— secular as well as Christian—and individuals themselves, especially the young.

The young.

Satan's punching bags, so to speak.

Assaulted by liberal teachers at secular schools, teachers who might not lay a hand on them but who grabbed control of their minds by humanistic and related teachings, by disguised nihilistic philosophy, by "tools" useful in breaking down their morals and their ethics.

Young people who then, unimpeded by righteousness, got out and spread violence, immorality and more.

"We should continually pray for the solidarity of strong Christ-centered schools," Darien remarked.

"Until one or more of those start to fall into unfortunate circumstances as well," Stedfast said.

An instant later they arrived at their destination: Southwestern Baptist Theological Seminary.

Part I

Rather let my head stoop to the block, that these knees bow to any save to the God of heaven.

William Shakespeare

Chapter 1

The day of the massacre just a few miles away did not seem special to anyone of flesh and blood—no forebodings of gloom, no frantic e-mails exchanged, no last minute attempts to cancel the event at Wedgwood Baptist Church because someone called in a warning message hoping to avert the slaughter, for there were to be no such calls, no warnings, except for fallen and unfallen angels who would be at the scene, each playing out the role into which destiny had forced them.

No ominous thunderclaps could be heard, loud as only Texas could find them, nor flashes of lightning seen skipping across the land, no shaking of the earth beneath finite feet; rather the sky clear, and present a kind of peace that seemed ironic in view of what was to follow.

Not that type of day at all, implicit with any sort of starkly prophetic clues that could have been gleaned by those experienced in such matters.

It was clear this day, a pleasant one as it started out, a day when sweltering temperatures were beginning to decrease after the onslaught of summer heat typical of the Fort Worth area.

Several students had come to the garden area, its *koi* pond spanned by an Oriental-style bridge, with a man-made waterfall at one end. At the edge, in the middle, stood a bronze statue of Jesus the Fisherman.

Quiet, seemingly isolated, yet surrounded by three key buildings: Student Center, Truett and Price Hall.

This was a place cherished, a special place given to Bible study and contemplation, with a large gazebo and several benches placed around the perimeter so that students and a not unsurprising number of faculty members could sit, think, offer up prayers to an overseeing Creator, and come away from the garden with their minds clear, their bodies relaxed, their souls refreshed.

One wedding had been held at the garden, and others were sure to follow, for it was romantic there, and uncommonly inspiring; the perfect spot for those in love to start a new life together.

And mourners from nearby funerals would nurse their sorrow amidst the quietude after leaving the graveside elsewhere and coming to that spot.

It was not difficult for many visitors to recall a certain hymn while looking at the trees, often at night when few others were present, trees that seemed transformed as moonlight danced across their leaves; or perhaps during early morning when only the sound of a multitude of various kinds of birds just awakening and calling to one another could be heard.

I come to the garden alone....

To praise Almighty God, yes, and always that, alone to appreciate the bounty of a loving Creator, His Son and an indwelling Holy Spirit, these blessings manifold only from Heaven itself.

And He tells me I am His own.

A familiar voice seemed to speak within the soul, whispering like the trees, stirred by the gentlest of breezes.

And the joy we share as we tarry there.

Joy.

The garden was a place of joy.

Quiet joy, not the sort that engenders boisterous outbursts but softer, sweeter, perhaps more real.

Sometimes arms were outstretched, hands upward, eyes closed, heads tilted back, as though in sync with Heaven; sometimes none of this happening, just a simple but profound surrender to quietude.

Kim Jones and Shawn Brown came often to this most special place, sat in the midst of its obvious inherent serenity and felt the refreshing of themselves that it invariably provided. Sydney Browning may have also; though it was created after she had graduated, it was so charming that word certainly would have spread, surely beckoning her to its promises.

Not a worshiping of nature, not the delusion that the garden had a kind of New Age aura about it!

But Christian men and women simply wanted to be where the surroundings gave them a chance to relax, to meditate on Scripture, to pray to the God they loved with everything that they were, often to thank Him for the matchless sacrifice of His only begotten Son, a sacrifice that allowed the redemption of their souls that they knew as a reality of their lives.

And then the day began in earnest, separation surrendering to an involvement with the sort of life chosen by most of the garden visitors.

Students, deans and professors alike left the garden and went to their offices, their classrooms.

Empty.

For a time, the garden was empty, except for the *koi* and the birds…until someone came with a need to be there, a need to experience the serendipity that was its greatest treasure.

Knowing the area as he undoubtedly did—else how could Larry Ashbrook have found out-of-the-way Wedgwood Baptist?— if he perchance had stopped by one day or at night, had bowed his head in agony, had prayed earnestly, coming to God in his suffering, whether emotional, psychological, spiritual or a combination of all, this man soon-to-die might not have done what he was planning to do from the moment he left his bed that morning.

No one else could have guessed, could have predicted, not in the garden, nor in the rest of the campus at Southwestern Baptist Theological Seminary, nowhere in that whole area was there any hint of the coming nightmare, nowhere except in the mind of a man who was to let loose with rage so red-hot in its intensity that not psychology alone could explain it.

September 15, 1999.

Just hours before the bloody holocaust that would sweep through Wedgwood Baptist Church.

Chapter 2

John MacArthur delivered a stirring sermon at the 1500-seat Truett Auditorium that morning just after 10:00.

A quieter sort of preacher when compared to others perhaps, he nevertheless captured the attention of everyone there on September 15, 1999, faculty sitting together with students, listening to a man who was dedicated to the truth even when that truth was not particularly fashionable, even when it could be prone to stirring up controversy for one reason or another.

John MacArthur was a man of depth.

If someone such as Larry Ashbrook could have heard this man, could have opened his demon-beset mind up to what was being said, John MacArthur might have become God's instrument in reaching his troubled mind and spirit, for he had a long history of helping those who were spiritually oppressed, even those with the deepest psychological problems.

Through the wisdom of God, that was not to be, of course, but it was joined by a long list of besetting *what ifs* that would plague the faculty and students of Southwestern Baptist Theological Seminary and the staff of Wedgwood Baptist, plague them for a very long time to come once the nightmare had been manifested. They would return to where they lived, dorm or apartment or private home, their bodies shaking, trembling, crying, barely able to stand, some indeed collapsing and having to be assisted the rest of the way, their minds shouting, "Oh, God, God, God, God," but not in any profane way; more a prayer, a soul-deep prayer acknowledging their human inability to deal with the worst shock of lives spent at the foot of the cross, a shock for those who were present, of course, but as well for others not there at the time...friends dead at the hands of a murderer, friends wounded, friends terrorized, the blood of the innocent flowing on holy ground.

Just hours away.

So it was that the two angels stood outside the main entrance to Southwestern Baptist Theological Seminary and viewed the mammoth domed building ahead of them, the organizational and architectural hub of the entire seminary, which was vibrant with activity.

And from there they would go to an altogether different location.

Wedgwood Baptist Church.

A large brick building that seemed so much a contrast to the residences on all sides of it.

"A tomb," Darien spoke with great solemnity, feeling the angelic equivalent of a chill.

Stedfast was silent, lost in the thoughts that that description engendered in his angelic mind.

"The odor of blood is pure imagination," Darien continued, "I know that, but I do seem to sense it already, Stedfast, almost as something quite palpable. We have detected it before at other places of tragedy around the world, but never more blatantly than right here."

"Surely we must warn them," the other angel protested. "Surely this massacre cannot be—"

"Did God tell us to do that?" Darien rebuked him, though not so sternly as he might have.

Stedfast hesitated but then felt compelled to speak further.

"No," the angel acknowledged, "but are we to stand by and watch this tragedy play out before us?"

"We must not do what Almighty God has forbidden," Darien reminded his ancient comrade.

Stedfast knew the answer as well as Darien did, but the enormity of it was not easily borne.

"But seven will die," he spoke with great emotion.

"Stedfast?" replied Darien.

"Yes?"

"What are you doing?"

Stedfast hesitated yet again, then said sheepishly, "I know, I know, dear friend, but it is difficult."

"I agree, but, eons ago, endless questions without answers were what gave birth to evil."

They had known the former Lucifer while he was still in Heaven, heard this most splendid of angels voice his doubts, heard those doubts grow in number and depth until he who was to become satan the prince of darkness gave up everything that was good and decent.

"His countenance!" Stedfast recalled. "Once so fine, the brilliance of a thousand suns."

No longer.

He was then a creature so loathsome that unfallen angels momentarily turned away from the sight of him as he fled past the gates, his band of fellow fallen ones mirror images of himself.

For a moment, the once majestic one turned and looked back, which all of the unfallen ones witnessed, and then he pulled more tightly a cloak of malevolence around himself, and was gone.

"Did Lucifer feel regret then?" Stedfast asked. "I have wondered about that since the Casting Out occurred."

"We may never know," Darien replied. "Though my suspicion is that Lucifer did, but regret was submerged beneath his ego and never allowed to assert any kind of control."

The next instant legions of those cast out surrendered to the perpetual infamy that would be their creation for the rest of time.

"So much death occurred for so very long," Stedfast mused with great weariness, "and now there is to be yet more, always more, this time seven innocent young people, their blood—"

He stopped, his countenance dimming, the angelic equivalent of crying now overwhelming him.

A lobby, with young people sitting to one side, ready to greet visitors in the name of Jesus.

A lobby soon to be the scene of the shedding of innocent blood.

Both angels were there momentarily.

And so was Sydney Browning, her own death but minutes away, the first SWBTS alumnus to be shot.

The first to die.

Chapter 3

Sydney Browning was not everybody's idea of a good friend, not by a long shot, as the expression went.

Some who met her went away shaking their heads, never wanting to see her again.

"We can't keep up with her," these individuals would say. "She's so cheerful all the time. We'd wear ourselves out emotionally if we were to try. But Sydney has the capacity to be 'up' many more times than down. We wish we were as fortunate as she is, but we're not."

A far larger group, though, found spending time with Sydney to be an invigorating and memorable experience.

She was not like all those people who smiled easily, seemed to be the life of the party and then, away from the spotlight, their true personalities were anything but the same.

Sydney did not change, cynically or otherwise.

There was never a hint of any kind of inherent pretense in this 36-year-young woman.

And she was someone most men would have dreamed of having as a wife someday?

Oh, yes, that.

Men searched for, longed for someone like Sydney, for she was what many would call ideal.

Yet she never married.

"I just haven't found anyone I would want to change my life for," she would say when asked about this.

...anyone I would want to change my life for.

But there were many who would change their lives for Sydney.

"No human being with a sin nature can ever be perfect," remarked a male friend about her age who would have been very happy to get know her better than he did. "But Sydney was everything that any reasonable person could have expected in a Christian woman."

And she had a really good sense of humor.

"When I get to Heaven," Sydney once remarked, a grin on her thin face, her voice filled with an unspoken peace, "I'll probably think, 'Now I can eat all the bleu cheese I want.'

"But I wonder if God's going to look at me and say, 'I gave you that to enjoy on earth, Sydney. You were worried about all the wrong things on earth there. You're not having bleu cheese here.'"

An innate cheerfulness.

And yet—

Despite the fact that when Sydney was around people, she would light up an entire room and become an instant beacon to anyone who saw her, despite an ability to get up on stage, any stage anywhere, perhaps during one of the daily chapel services at Southwestern Baptist Theological Seminary—where the audience could grow to more than a thousand men and women across a wide spectrum of ages and responsibilities, with deans, professors, visiting missionaries and students alike attending—get up there before them, yes, and have everybody all focus, rather, become riveted on her, despite all this and more, it was also true that she valued her "space," that she lived alone a thousand miles from her parents, and enjoyed most those plentiful times of solitude spent in communication with the Lord.

"Her close friends knew enough not to interrupt Sydney during any of those periods of aloneness," another student from the seminary remarked with great wistfulness. "If someone did intrude, without knowing the routine, so to speak, Sydney would be unfailingly pleasant, polite, that sort of thing, but this kind of situation was just not what she preferred.

"Some folks have said that cats are often aloof. Yet I have lived with cats all my life, and find them not to be like that except during those daily moments when they need to get off by themselves.

"Sydney was a little like that, you know, but, even so, when she was with a crowd, or even a pretty small group, she was just the opposite, celebrating life while reserving other periods for when she was on her knees, thanking God for the life that He had given her."

....thanking God for the life that He had given her.

That was what Sydney did.

Always, and ever.

Chapter 4

Success High School in Fort Worth was just 6.3 miles from SWBTS. In 15 minutes, with average traffic, she could go from one to the other.

A very large percentage of troubled students roamed its hallways, more than a few with criminal records and/or involved in gangs.

Sydney should not have had any rapport at all with them.

They were usually scruffy-looking, often profane, with a flippant manner toward authority, the children of *barrios* and/or broken homes, more than one of them involved in petty theft, drug dealing, robbery and whatever else they could find to fill their lives as a protest against what those lives had been like.

But she made it a point to avoid any semblance of the frustrating "should nots" of life.

"I believe that God enables us to be overcomers," this child of the King said again and again. "Triumph in Him...that's the only way I know of to approach any substantial challenge."

So Sydney seemed not to be fazed much by any of the tasks God set before her in life.

"She would always say that she never was afraid of *her* students because, after a year or so, she knew that they would not hurt her," remarked a friend.

To which her mother Diana Browning added, "If she got discouraged to any great degree, she never let us know."

And yet—

Her students.

Those were two words that made Sydney feel at peace with them while not like that with others because of an odd *impression* that entered her mind, an impression that she could not have known would be actually prophetic.

A shooting.

She sensed that it could come soon, whether a day, a week, a month ahead or longer, but felt odd thinking about it.

"I don't believe in premonitions or anything like that," she would say. "Instead I've wondered what the Lord was trying to tell me."

According to a friend, "It was the students she would never know who concerned her."

The track record of Success High School had not lived up to that word *success* nearly as well as it did shortly after Sydney arrived.

Not a coincidence.

During the two-and-a-half years she spent there, it became a place of rebirth for students under her influence, but, even so, for others it remained a place where anger exploded, where drugs were secretively bought and sold, a melting pot of the best of young people and the worst all under the same roof.

"I've never been one to wallow in regret, second-guessing, that sort of thing," she said a few weeks before the evening of September 15, 1999. "Yet I can't help but wish I could do more, reach more students. It's frustrating to see so many at Success High School and know in the center of my soul that large numbers will end up in jail or dead because of gunshots or overdoses or whatever else."

...because of gunshots.

That was how Sydney assumed any attempt on her life would be made, a gun fired by another student, one of the many whose life she had not as yet touched with her witness as a Christian.

Where exactly?

She wondered about that.

Perhaps out in the school parking lot or as she walked down a corridor or alone in her classroom as she graded papers.

But the attempt might have been by a knife, easier to hide and potentially just as lethal.

Quite a contrast to what Sydney perceived as the near-century-long security of SWBTS.

A cocoon, in a way, or a special world.

A *Christian* world separated from the outside influences of nihilism, paganism and the rest that had eaten away at American culture for so long.

Southwestern Baptist Theological Seminary was a world in which nearly 4000 students were the fortunate citizens, a world in many ways that seemed a boot camp of sorts, a boot camp preparing its Christian soldiers for the society beyond, and the ultimate destination of Heaven beyond that.

Peace.

Sydney would search it out while a student at SWBTS, search it out at chapel service filled with singing and preaching and student plays and more besides, or sometimes sitting inside when it was more or less empty.

Or in her dorm room, as she sat with her Bible, periodically bowing in prayer when a particular verse ministered to her.

Back at Success High School, true to form, Sydney did get through the initial rush of fear that assaulted her, which was remarkable since it was fear that made her look at the many students of Success High School and wonder which one would make an attempt on her life.

Pure fear...

On one level, yes, of course, that of not knowing, the mystery of when and how based upon the reality of the personal histories of so many students crammed together in one place.

And yet not fear of dying, not that at all.

"Whenever the Lord calls me home, I'll be ready"—that was Sydney's philosophy.

...I'll be ready.

Which was why she seemed constantly active in trying to accomplish something for the Cause of Christ, not paying lip service to those words while enjoying the kind of social life that was endemic to any institution of higher education.

Accomplish something....

For example: Being named Teacher of the Year.

This happened for Sydney at Success High School not long after she started teaching there.

"She won the honor the next year also," a family member would tell a journalist months later. "And she was about to have this repeated again the year after that, but she declined, wanting another dedicated teacher to be recognized."

Her strong faith was obvious to anyone who spent a few minutes or a few hours with her.

Let your light shine....

Letting this heaven-born light radiate from her had been a way of life for the 36-year-old.

Ever since Sydney was a child of just nine years in fact, but it was never "put on," a contrivance to impress those around her, an act as phony as any amateur stage performance.

Your light....

That light, that faith, that single-minded dedication kept Sydney going far longer than any long-lasting battery-powered bunny on a TV commercial, and she never allowed it to waver, in the midst of "off" days as well as those during which she felt at the top of her form, as the expression goes.

As might be suspected, some students were to be won over. Others were lost.

Later, members from both groups would attend Sydney Browning's exultant memorial service, brought together warily perhaps and shedding tears when they hoped no one was looking.

Chapter 5

Apart from the beauty of her personality, there was another factor that helped Sydney Browning "connect" with so many others during the latter course of her 36 years of life.

Her voice, distinctly fine.

When she spoke, that voice seemed to have a natural calming effect on whomever she was addressing, a gift enjoyed by few in a world where the frenetic seemed to rule daily.

"She could have been a world-class counselor if she had gone on in this life," remarked one of the other teachers at Success High School. "Parents took to her; so did students."

The teacher attempted a smile but failed, only a steady flow of tears evident instead.

"The steady, happy personality that Sydney projected was the reason," she added wistfully, "and a large part of *that* was the tender, caring sound of her voice, unforgettable."

...the tender, caring sound of her voice.

Unforgettable.

Oh, that it was, that it was indeed.

As far as Sydney's vocal ability was concerned, the effect that it invariably had on those with whom she spoke did not end there, through conversations complex or simple.

Singing.

Sydney enjoyed singing.

To say that she seemed to possess the voice of an angel was hardly an exaggeration.

And she never tired of one song/hymn, never tired of the inspired words, the melody, never tired of the impact it had upon those who were listening, an impact that turned their attention to the Father.

"Many angels must have gathered around, unseen," commented another appreciative member of Wedgwood Baptist, "gathered around and, yes, listened to dear Sydney each time she sang it, each time she put her heart and soul into the message that it embodied."

I'll Fly Away.

It was a song that seemed Sydney's trademark, a song that was everything she herself had proven to be over the 36 years of her life, beautiful and inspiring, helping the listener to soar spiritually, to look upward and almost, it seemed, to approach the very gates of heaven.

Like a bird from prison bars has flown....

Which she did the evening of September 15, 1999, at Wedgwood Baptist Church as mortal life fled her fragile form.

"Such a very nice, intelligent young lady," Stedfast observed, his sorrow nearly palpable. "If we could have been assigned to Sydney Browning for any length of time, we could surely have expected some joyous moments, dear friend. And yet, soon, a wave of sorrow so—"

He stopped, emotions controlling him.

"Indeed that is right," agreed Darien, then stopped, listening, his attention directed elsewhere.

"What is it?"

"That voice...."

Stedfast listened, and heard, heard a voice, a voice so special that if he had been of flesh and blood instead of pure spirit and could cry, he would have done no less, tears of joy.

"Yes..." he said, deeply affected.

He could do nothing but join with fellow angel Darien in appreciating the beauty of it.

"From another time, another place."

"Praise God for flashing us back in time, to that morning when she sang before the congregation."

"So very fine, this voice, so very—"

He stopped communicating and continued listening.

"Like the voice of an angel, Darien, like one of us," added Stedfast, and then he, too, was silent.

After Sydney Browning had finished her solo, the two angels continued their dialogue.

"That is so rare, Stedfast, a voice of such undeniable sweetness," Darien remarked. "This young woman, this fine young woman, if she were to live, could entertain and inspire many, many people over the years ahead. What a ministry of music she would have had."

But they knew the truth, the truth as God had revealed it to them, as the only source of true truth they had ever known.

"Lives touched by her great gift," Stedfast agreed. "But none of that will happen. Why, Darien, why, my dear friend?"

The other angel could not answer, in part because he was observing a beautiful scene.

"Look at the people...their eyes," he pointed out.

Sydney's audience.

"They have heard a touch of Heaven, though they cannot quite describe what that is," Stedfast said, "and they have been blessed."

"And the song, Stedfast...."

"Yes, yes...'I'll Fly Away'...her favorite actually."

"May she sing it often in Heaven when she passes the gates, and never tire of doing so."

Both angels turned from Sydney Browning, as their attention was directed by the God who created them and whom they loved, to another, away from the recent past to the present in the lobby of Wedgwood Baptist Church.

Kim Jones.

Chapter 6

A number of months after Kim Jones died when Larry Ashbrook fired a pistol at the back of her head, sending her into eternity, a family member sat in a small conference room at Southwestern Baptist Theological Seminary and cried, cried over the death of a daughter with such a happy personality that she commanded attention wherever she went.

Vibrant....

Somehow that seemed inadequate, a word that failed to describe with any kind of completeness the sort of young woman Kim became during the three-year period since she had accepted Jesus Christ as Savior and Lord. But then human words had their limitations when called upon to create an image of the spiritual.

Those who knew this remarkable young person could attest to the fact that she typically experienced fewer "down" times than anybody else they had ever known before Kim entered their lives.

Grief....

The tears shed were from more than what might be called an "average" sort of grief, for hers was based upon the unrelenting savagery of what happened on September 15, 1999.

"It is one thing to lose your child in an automobile accident, certainly a sudden, horrible way for her to be taken from you," she said, tears flowing. "It is yet another to lose a child to disease, disease perhaps coming slowly, the months dragging by as you can only stand to one side, and see your beloved slipping away. But having her taken from you while she is still vibrant and healthy, the very best years of her life ahead, that is harder, so much harder.

"Someone I never met was destined to come and change our lives forever," the family member remarked, her voice breaking, while trying to hang onto the forgiveness she was attempting to continue feeling for Larry Ashbrook, a forgiveness mandated by the death.

"I have learned how important it is to treasure every moment we have with a loved one. It's not money, not power or position or anything like that that any longer seems important. It's time, time spent with them, as much time as we can manage."

....having her taken from you while she is still vibrant and healthy.

Memories flooded in on her, including those associated with one of two major turning points in Kim's brief lifetime.

"She was always a child in love with life," she remarked, "until something happened."

...until something happened.

That something occurred when one of her friends accidentally shot his twin brother.

"I think it was a point in her life when she began hardening her heart," she added. "Instead of turning to God, as I prayed daily that she would, my daughter ran away from Him."

Rebellion.

A life of quite open rebellion, one that would last until three years before her death.

But Kim did not look the part of a rebel. She was a good student, not one who paid little attention to school altogether.

Friends.

She had an enviable number of solid friendships within the student body and outside it. At one point she was elected vice president of the student council at Klein High School in Spring, Texas.

And she befriended other students.

Kim went on to study at Texas Christian University. But she also got involved as a member of the Delta Gamma sorority and into partying pretty heavily.

She looked happy on the outside but, inside, she began to realize that something was wrong.

"The more I tried to find fulfillment in a life apart from God, the more miserable I became," she wrote in her SWBTS application during the month of June 1999. "I desperately wanted to be truly happy, to change myself, to become a better person but it wasn't happening."

Years ago, at the time she was so unsettled, those last few words would have had a note of desperation.

"By the time I was 20, I had made a huge mess of my life," Kim would acknowledge. "When I looked in the mirror, I was ashamed of the person I had become. I was empty and broken, chasing after the things of the world."

Kim was fortunate, though.

Threads of the faith with which her parents had raised her steadfastly survived this transitory period of rebellion. If the deceiver had begun to detect the scent of victory in a moment of his own deception, a deception that told him he would be given yet another soul on Planet Earth, he would have it snatched from him before Kim could be dealt any lingering damage.

"I fell to my knees in 1996, close to Halloween," she said, with a bit of a grin on her face as she considered the irony of her rededication to Christ just before a holiday with its implicit satanic core, yet "accepted" by many Christian parents with little regard for or awareness of its origins, "and I begged Him, 'Lord, if You are real, and You are true, then, please, please change me.' "

From the center of her soul.

….*please, please change me.*

Brokenness.

That was a moment of indelible brokenness for Kim.

"At that moment, as I bowed before the throne of grace, I met Jesus as never before, and He changed everything about me."

A longtime friend later said of Kim Jones, "She did completely surrender every aspect of her life to the Lord. I've never met someone like her....She loved Jesus Christ incorruptibly."

"Kim was someone who desired to share Christ because God had so transformed her life by His love that she wanted everyone to know the precious life that was now hers," a friend of hers recalled. "She would go to the Clinique counter at a local department store to receive a makeover in order to have the opportunity to talk about the Lord with a makeup artist.

"Last fall, after sharing her testimony and the plan of salvation with one of them, she did become concerned because she was unable to completely explain salvation before the makeover was finished.

"The next day, Kim went back to speak with the same individual again but discovered that the person was not at work. Instead of just leaving, she decided to leave a note that read:

" 'Nothing seemed to make me feel happy or at last fulfilled until I asked Jesus to come into my heart and change me. My prayer for you is that one day you could meet Jesus and experience His love, peace and joy...and then one day I would see you in heaven.'"

Joy.

That was at the center of Kim's existence after she accepted Jesus Christ as her Savior, her Lord.

"The Christian life should be a life full of joy," she wrote in what might be called an essay about being saved, "full of hope, full of meaning, full of everything. Jesus wants to give us life worth living, not only here but in eternity.

"You've got to spend time in God's Word...You've got to read the Bible and spend time in prayer and seek His will. The Lord wants us to love Him with all of our heart, with all of our soul, with all of our mind. He wants us to walk with Him daily, not just when we're at church."

Kim closed that document with the following prayer: "Dear God, I just come before You, and I ask that You would touch each person's heart…[who hears these words]…Lord, help us to live a life of purpose, and with meaning. Lord, help us to live a life that is going to count for eternity.

"Lord, just give us life abundantly. Help us to stop holding on to the things that are going to perish, but, instead, to store up our treasures in heaven. God, help us to do that…God, do so much more than we could ever ask or could ever know. In the precious, most holy name of Jesus…Amen."

Chapter 7

Just two days before her death....

Kim made what turned out to be her very last entry in a journal that she had been keeping for quite some time: "I don't want to ever lose the passion of being totally in love with You alone! God, please continue to stir my heart, make me passionate now and always."

As far as she was concerned, being a Christian meant giving God a hundred percent.

"Anything less is not good enough," Kim wrote. "I will feel this way regardless of whatever the circumstances might be—"

She added some words that seem prophetic in view of what was to happen just two days later.

"....even if my walk with God is ever to cost me my life."

A sense of impending martyrdom.

Those who knew Kim well—including her mother—claimed that she was not prone to grim foreboding.

And yet—

A statement by Kim to a close friend had been made two months earlier that offered a clue.

"I think it would be the greatest honor to die for Christ," she remarked after reading a book entitled *Through Gates of Splendor* about five missionaries martyred in South America.

Two instances of Kim speaking about death.

Coincidence, or something more?

A to-the-point title of one of the Bible studies she led in a Middle Eastern country where her parents were living at the time provided perhaps additional insight into what motivated Kim, a title that was as well an admonition: *Are you living a life that counts for eternity?*

"She was so dedicated," a fellow student at SWBTS recalled. "The rest of us were drawn to her, for she was the greatest role model imaginable."

Here was how Darren J. Middleton, assistant professor of religion at Texas Christian University described her during the time of study she spent there: "I came to understand that Kim's pursuit of a credible and livable faith was as impressive as it was relentless.

"The end result of her labors was just shy of mesmeric...I remember admiring the way she had trained her mind and heart to consider important issues about life, meaning and God.

"Today as I ponder the tragic loss of Kim's young and tender life, I find myself celebrating her transparently honest Christianity. I don't mind admitting that I am a better theologian for having met Kim Jones; in her own extravagantly gracious way, she taught me more than I could say here or anywhere."

Losing someone so fine would hurt, a loss that none of her loved ones and friends could have suspected was impending, a light in the darkness, a light suddenly extinguished.

"To go from a life of momentary rebellion to one of submission by her own choice and with unqualified love," Stedfast remarked. "We have seen many like her over the centuries but few more impressive, few more on fire for the truth that can come only from the Bible, God's Word."

Darien was silent, which was hardly typical of him.

"Do you not agree?" Stedfast asked.

"I do, of course, I do," the other angel replied, almost absentminded in his manner.

Darien paused yet again, then: "You know, dear comrade, I never tire of knowing that transformations like this happen, of witnessing each one, of—"

Stedfast felt the same way.

"It is one of the joys of our existence," he said, " to watch a soul turn from darkness to light."

"The old things are passed away, just like the new heaven and the earth taking over from the old."

"It is obvious that Kim Jones engenders love from everyone she meets," Stedfast added.

Being Christ-like.

That was a definition of the word "Christian," and Kim embodied its meaning more than Christians supposedly far more mature in their walk with Him.

"She has a trusting personality," Darien added, "one that reaches out and draws people to her."

Energy.

An energy of the soul that was manifested in the physically and emotionally dynamic personality that was hers.

It was not the ridiculous kind that was introduced by New Agers but something quite different from that, an energy born of vibrant youth and growing familiarity with all that God expected of her, and a sense of true self, not of ego but, rather, appreciation, appreciation to God for the very breath of life given to her long before she left her adoring mother's womb.

"If only she could have continued this way," Stedfast said.

"Think of the wife she could have been, the mother," Darien spoke, "but she will never have the opportunity, never—"

"I do not know if I can stay," Stedfast admitted to his comrade, "if I shall be able to—"

He turned away briefly, turned away from that sanctuary, turned away from seeing those creatures of flesh and blood soon to shed their mortal frames, those souls soon to be taken to heaven.

There could be no tears from this angel—from whence would these come?—but that made his sorrow all the more oppressive since he had no human-like release for it, none at all.

There was darkness ahead, the darkness of unrelieved pure evil that would sweep over Kim Jones, Sydney Browning, Shawn Brown and four others. If the two angels had been of flesh and blood, they would have felt the chill of it, the soon-to-be terror of that night.

But neither could leave just yet, for God would have them meet someone else, the third martyr.

Shawn Brown.

Chapter 8

Braveheart, Big Heart.

That was what one article in *Southwestern News* dubbed Shawn Brown a short while after his death.

In some respects he seemed more a young man destined for an acting career than one in the ministry. One journalist, formerly Hollywood-based, but now a member of the SWBTS faculty, came to this conclusion after seeing some photos of him, his evaluation resting on more than 30 years of interviewing movie and TV talent, established actors and newcomers alike.

"Shawn seems to have had the physical ingredients to make it big," he offered. "If he could act, then the combination might have taken him far, though, on the other hand, it is likely that the doggedly anti-Christian lifestyles and compromises endemic to Hollywood would have been very frustrating to somebody like Shawn, driving him out of the industry in short order unless by the sheer persuasiveness of his personality and what he had to say, Shawn could have become a force for redemption, as he did everywhere he went."

...everywhere he went.

In an era of stone-faced movie heroes, Shawn would have been a more than acceptable alternative. But acting probably never entered his mind. He was interested only in one goal.

Serving his Lord.

"He was the real deal," remarked Scott Copeland, a friend. "People found it easy to have confidence in him, to be themselves around Shawn."

This 23-year-old was especially interested in starting a ministry aimed at struggling teenagers.

"Shawn's heart definitely was for youth ministry," Kathy Jo, his wife of nearly three years, observed, "and he really enjoyed going to Christian garage band concerts to visit with them."

And he was creative in how he tried to "reach" young people.

According to *Southwestern News*, "When a girl said that she was having trouble learning to give thanks regularly to God, Shawn went right away and told her to take one of her shoes and throw it into the air to symbolize letting go of her problem and giving it all to the Lord. Soon thereafter, that same girl was able to thank God with much greater ease.

"Another time, Shawn challenged his youth group at First Baptist Church of Bronte, Texas, to get 60 people to come to a Wednesday night service, promising that if they did, he would shave his head and grow a long goatee.

"They went out and did exactly that, and Shawn kept his promise. For teenagers to understand and take the Gospel to heart, he believed they had to understand it in a unique way."

...in a unique way.

He approached soul-winning with a certain urgency.

"We can't waste time," Shawn once said, "because we never know how much is left for one person or another. I always feel an urgency when I see someone in need of salvation."

This was illustrated by one instance that involved Shawn leading a woman to Jesus two days before she died of a heart attack.

"He was so glad that he had taken the opportunity before it slipped away," a friend recalled, "so glad that he had avoided personal convenience and heeded the leading of the Holy Spirit."

This woman entered Heaven undoubtedly to the accompaniment of a chorus of angels bidding her welcome.

"What joy Shawn will experience when he sees her," Stedfast observed.

"It is a joy he deserves," agreed Darien. "But there will be others, gathered around, waiting for him."

Shawn did not minister because he wanted to be repaid, as it were, by joy. He cared little about the results of his efforts as they concerned himself but primarily as those results affected others.

"He wanted to change the direction of the lives of young people who were in trouble," Darien added.

"I heard him at night, sometimes in anguish that he had not done enough for the Lord that day," Stedfast recalled, "one soul crying out for the chance to be an instrument of salvation for others."

"You felt a special rapport with him, did you not?"

"Oh, yes, Darien. I went back in time a few years and saw what he was like early on.

"He never changed, did he?"

"Never."

Chapter 9

Shawn related well to older adults with equal impact.

"He could run the whole gamut," Jason Bruce, a friend, pointed out. "Shawn was a kid at heart. He loved to joke around and goof off, but he could also come to the level of a senior adult."

It was at Southwestern Baptist Theological Seminary that Shawn was to have his most fulfilling moments and where he undoubtedly would reach the most people, partly because it was the largest such institution in the world, and its thousands of students from scores of different countries and of a variety of ages offered him the best opportunities for relationships.

"Above all," Kathy Jo said, "my husband loved learning here. He joked that we were getting a two-for-one deal" because he was eager to tell her about what he had learned in class.

Just 24 hours before he died, he spent time at home with his wife, talking about an upcoming West Texas youth rally.

"I have so much to share, I don't know where to start," he told Kathy Jo, hugging her with great affection.

Shawn was gifted with a singular ability.

"He knew how to make you know what you felt deeply was important," she remarked. "He cared about people. He was always ready to counsel or listen. He took all this seriously."

...all this seriously.

1) Leading people to the Lord.

2) Making sure that he was able always to project the right testimony as a beacon to others.

3) Learning more and more about the Bible so that he would have more to share with others.

All of these were the bits and pieces of a life dedicated to spreading the Good News.

Kissing the cold head of such a young man as his body rested in a coffin would be the hardest act Kathy Jo would ever perform because Shawn was so exceptional that filling the void his death left in her life would ultimately prove the greatest challenge she could possibly face.

Shawn's stance on marriage was uncompromising.

"My friend was a very big believer in having a proper marriage and a right relationship with his wife," commented Jason Bruce. "Whenever he would hear about spouses cheating on each other, or ending their marriages, Shawn would become irritated big-time."

Kathy Jo and Shawn became husband and wife a bit less than two years before he died.

Children.

Becoming parents was a goal this young couple wanted very much, a legacy they would have cherished.

"Everything seemed so wonderful for the two of us," she recalled. "It was like a real-life fairy tale for the two of us, with every piece fitting in place as though set there by an unseen Hand."

Kathy Jo paused, then smiled wistfully as she added, "And Jesus Christ was at the center of our lives."

...at the center of our lives.

Nothing could be said more accurately: prayer times at home throughout each day; regular Bible reading and study; church services on Sunday as well as Wednesday evening; witnessing to people everywhere they went, whether they did this individually or as a couple.

Shawn had a personal life verse: It was First Timothy 4:16 (NIV): "Watch your life and doctrine closely. Persevere in them, because if you do, you will save both yourself and your hearers."

After the funeral, Kathy Jo wrote the following letter to the SWBTS family she and Shawn treasured: "I am so thankful for you and your love during the loss of my precious husband."

She fought back tears as she added, "Shawn loved being a student at [SWBTS]....He would be pleased to know that many young men and women will continue to benefit through the Shawn C. Brown Scholarship Fund.

"I have truly been overwhelmed as God has taken care of me through friends and loved ones like you. All of the sweet cards, prayers, and words of comfort have ministered to me tremendously."

She smiled sadly yet radiantly at the same time.

"I am so thankful for the blessing of being Shawn's wife, and I rejoice in the fact that I will get to be with him again one day," Kathy added. "Thanks to God's awesome faithfulness, and His promise in Romans 8:28, many others will be with us in Heaven as well—those who have come to know Christ through this tragedy.

"May we continue seeking God and leading others to Christ, so as to not let the loss of our Shawn be in vain. It is my prayer, that we would 'run with perseverance the race marked out for us.' (Hebrews 12:1-3) as Shawn desired to share at an upcoming youth rally.

"May God bless you.

"In Christ's eternal love,

"Kathy Jo Brown."

Both angels marveled at the selfless and energetic dedication that characterized Shawn Brown.

"He had everything ahead of him," Darien observed, "a wife with whom he was deeply in love, and who was devoted to him as well."

"They were enjoying so beautiful a relationship, the sort of relationship that our kind will never know," Stedfast pointed out, *"and yet acting completely in accordance with Scripture, as husband and wife."*

"Think of it."

"Of what, Darien?"

"They could have had children and grandchildren and perhaps great grandchildren, and so much else in their lives."

"Unlike our kind."

Set apart.

Angels were every bit that.

And they shared a certain commonality with human beings.

"They and we are God's children, Stedfast. We were spoken into existence from the very mind of our Creator."

"I wonder, though, how it would have been if—"

Darien would not hear any of what he anticipated the other angel was about to say, aware as he was of his comrade's propensity for analyzing and re-analyzing over and over.

"Settled at the beginning of time and eternity," he spoke impatiently. *"No need to revisit it now."*

His manner softened.

"Be as your name, dear Stedfast, be as your name."

The other angel hesitated, then said, "It should be yours, true friend, yes, it should be yours."

Part II

Nothing can prepare us for the advent of death, not all the well-intended reassurances of life everlasting, nothing that could ever be spoken or read, for death is dark, dank, cruel. Only that which comes instantly after, the light of heaven, the singing of a multitude of angels, the fulfilled promises of God's Word, only this can allow us to say goodbye to the fear and live the glory.

Anonymous

Chapter 10

Just before the Wedgwood Baptist assignment, Darien and Stedfast had been with a multitude of persecuted Christian brothers and sisters in a foreign land thousands of miles away.

But now both had gone on to the United States, a free country where worship was supposed to be a Constitutional-mandated right.

The two unfallen angels at once saw the other side of worship, not under the ruthless dictatorial attention of a government committed to stamping out Christianity but, rather, freedom that could be pursued freely, with great joy, and an accompanying peace of mind.

"But the outcome will be the same tonight," Stedfast moaned, "the same as though this was a country under the control of a dictator."

Darien understood the irony of that.

"It would have been so fine to get to know their mothers and fathers better," Darien suggested warmly.

They had already been in the company of Kim's mother, an attractive, emotional woman who was devoted to her daughter.

"She is such a fine lady," Stedfast spoke. "She seemed almost to know that we were there."

"I have seldom seen such sensitivity," Darien added. "But she definitely had it, I agree, Stedfast."

"And Shawn's wife...lovely woman."

77

"Yes, she is...with a very pleasant voice, like that of a child...I enjoyed hearing her speak."

"And the others...exceptional young people coming from the most wonderful families."

Stedfast hesitated, his luminescence flickering for an instant, an angelic sign of indecision.

"Go ahead," Darien prompted.

He was aware that his friend wanted to say something but was uncommonly reluctant.

"Darien?" Stedfast ventured again.

"Yes, Stedfast?"

"Why here? Tonight?"

He paused, then added, "With no way to change the ghastly night-mare that is just ahead."

"Should we not have been introduced earlier in their lives?" added Darien forlornly.

"I have no idea but we both can agree that God has never made a mistake nor had a lapse of judgment, not from the beginning of our rela-tionship with Him up to this very moment."

"Listen...."

"To what?"

"Muttering...I hear someone muttering."

"In this building?"

"No, outside...he seems to be struggling."

In an instant they were outside, and it was there, as he walked toward the sanctuary, that they met someone else.

A man.

Just getting out of his pickup truck.

Larry Ashbrook.

They saw him, thought nothing of him until he strode toward the sanctuary, until they saw his eyes, the language of his body.

"Darien?" asked Stedfast.

"Do not speak now," Darien told him.

They both felt a kind of chill, not the sort that grabbed human beings but that which was more profoundly unsettling.

"Strange man," Stedfast observed.

"Indeed he is," Darien said, "but we must not judge by outward appearances, my friend."

The two angels were in the large well-filled parking lot of Wedgwood Baptist Church.

"I do not think—," Stedfast started to say.

One hand was jammed deep into his right jeans pocket.

Both angels, while knowing his mission, still felt a degree of shock and horror that was not much different from what would have been the case if they had been totally ignorant of it.

This one, this missionary of pain and death, this puppet of evil, was not alone. He had companions, unseen to mortal eyes but still present, at his side, whispering, nudging, urging.

Darien and Stedfast saw them, every last loathsome, perverse, grotesque creature, each a demon there who had once been a cherished companion along the golden streets of Heaven.

"We once were so happy together," Stedfast lamented.

"History could have been so very different," Darien joined him in mourning what once was.

A confrontation was coming.

It could not be avoided, though the two angels sent by God knew the outcome as He had revealed it to them.

Still of luminescent brilliance.

Filled with glorious color that was their "birthright."

Darien and Stedfast approached the others.

The others....

So difficult even to look at what they had become.

Chapter 11

"If I were of flesh and blood," Stedfast whispered with great despair, "I would be...I would be—"

"Sick, yes," Darien interpolated, "which is as I feel. May we have the strength to speak with them."

"I do not know, my friend; they are at once disgusting and pathetic, driven by their enslavement."

Fallen ones.

Demonic entities.

Hovering.

Out of flesh-and-blood sight.

But present nevertheless.

One of them was laughing.

"Ah, you have been sent here!" he exclaimed heartily. "Now what in the world could your mission be, my former comrades? As for us, we are quite aware of what ours is."

Darien knew this one, knew him from that era when he was still in Heaven, still a member of the loyal multitudes obedient to their Creator, worshiping Him, adoring Him.

Nupain.

"You are here without your master," Darien said with intentional sarcasm. *"Did they finally decide to let you go out on your own? I thought that you were being confined strictly to hell."*

Darien had witnessed Nupain just once in the outer reaches of that dismal place of unending torment, but it was once, this fleeting glimpse, to make him want to reach out and somehow—

Not to be, not to be, not to be.

"I could hardly fulfill my potential there," Nupain snorted, his ego as ghastly as his appearance.

"And what is your potential?"

"To enjoy the pain of mortals, to inflict it whenever possible."

"No longer the already damned?"

"That was merely a stage in my development...I am capable of so much more, Darien."

"How you must have rankled at the pain of the dying and the diseased enjoyed by your so-called comrades as they immersed themselves in wars and pestilence and murder and rape and all the rest, while you were assigned to the predictable routines of hell. No challenges there! The damned could not resist you, Nupain."

Darien could tell that his words were getting through to the fallen creature in front of him.

"But here, in the finite realm, you actually could be rejected, think of that!" he exclaimed. *"My oh my, Nupain, you could find yourself facing a subject who actually turns his back on you, who chooses instead his loving God of Heaven rather than your evil satan of hell."*

Nupain, though, feigned a certain smugness.

"Chatter on as you wish," he said, *"for you have little time remaining for that pious prattle of yours."*

He summoned the other creatures to stand in line behind him.

"Darien?" asked Stedfast.

"Yes?" Darien replied.

"Could we not petition God? Could we not—?"

"He would communicate with us if He was to decide otherwise. And, you know, He has not."

Nupain overheard.

"*Frustrating, right?*" he spoke. "*Frustrating that you serve God who claims righteousness and then plunges you in this garbage.*"

Darien saw an opening.

"*Garbage?*" he repeated. "*Even you use that word?*"

"*I could think of no other,*" Nupain replied, "*though it seems hardly enough to convey the reality, the truth.*"

"*Then why? Why go ahead? Why destroy lives? Why feast on despair?*"

"*I have no choice. Satan controls us. With God, I had free will. With satan, there is no such thing. I can do nothing but that which he demands.*"

His cankered wings sagged, his already dismal countenance darkening all the more.

The other demons were looking at him with growing puzzlement, never having seen this side of their unholy comrade.

"*I shall go in there with Larry Ashbrook,*" Nupain said, trying to reassume an aura of leadership, "*and my kind and I will stir this man, this poor oppressed soul, into a frenzy.*"

He glanced at the other demons.

"*What we are is what we chose,*" he added, "*and what we chose is how we will be until the end of time and beyond. Every bit of misery we have inflicted on mortal humans we, too, shall suffer times ten.*"

Nupain came so close to Darien that their spirits almost blended.

"*Be grateful for your destiny,*" he spoke. "*Be grateful that you are not as we, alcoholics chained to a bottle, addicts to a needle, gamblers to slot machines and crap tables and whatever else.*

"*We were behind all of that, as you know, but, ironically, the alcoholics, the addicts, the others can change if they find the strength, the determination, once, yes, they turn to God.*"

He paused, then added, "*Not us, my dear Darien. The dice have already been rolled. And we await our doom.*"

He turned from Darien and, also, Stedfast, and they all, these evil creatures from the domain of hell, went with Larry Ashbrook into Wedgwood Baptist.

And there it began.

Chapter 12

In the days and weeks to follow, there would be many reports describing the escalation of violence and other events once Larry Ashbrook entered Wedgwood Baptist Church.

The basic details were as follows:

September 15, 1999:

6:40 p.m.—Rally commenced.

6:50 p.m.—Larry Ashbrook approached some welcoming young people in the lobby of Wedgwood Baptist Church. His first victim, Jeff Laster, was shot seconds later.

6:51 p.m.—Ashbrook shot Sydney Browning who was sitting on a couch to his right, waiting to welcome visitors; she died instantly.

6:51 p.m.— He shot and wounded Jaynanne Brown a bit less than a minute later.

6:52 p.m.—Ashbrook then noticed Kevin Galey approaching and wounded him with two shots.

6:55 p.m.—Entering the hallway adjacent to the visitors area to see what was going on, Mike Holton was fired upon twice, then dashed back into the library and was able to place the first 911 call.

6:58 p.m.—Ashbrook shot and killed Shawn Brown just outside the main sanctuary.

6:59 p.m.—He then entered the Wedgwood Baptist sanctuary and, in rapid succession, murdered Kim Jones, Cassie Griffin, Kristie Beckel, Joey Ennis and Steggy Ray—as well as wounding Justin Laird, Mary Beth Talley, Robert DeBord and Nicholas Skinner.

7:02 p.m.—After being confronted by Jeremiah Neitz, Larry Ashbrook shot and killed himself.

Approximately 12 minutes in all, a life taken every minute and a half, the wounded in puddles of blood.

Those were the basic "facts" regarding SWBTS's and Wedgwood's young people as victims. But there was much more going on within the church building, some of it seen, some sensed, some unseen.

Darien and Stedfast at first could be only observers. Figuratively speaking, their hands seemed to be tied by the commands of their Creator.

But just at first.

Within the next few minutes, they would have a great deal to do, along with other unfallen angels inside Wedgwood Baptist, angels whose mission was to save the lives of hundreds of other young people in attendance for the rally, plus safeguarding members of the staff of the church such as Jeff Fanin and Kevin Galey.

Yet, for Darien and Stedfast, there would be no ministry to the living, for it was instead the soon-dead to whom they were assigned.

Seven souls leaving useless bodies of flesh and blood.

One by one they passed from mortality to eternity.

Sydney Browning proved to be the first, Sydney of the musical personality and the lyrical voice, Sydney beloved by all who knew her, Sydney who if she could have had only a short while with even a man such as Larry Ashbrook might have changed him, might have saved his life along with those of his other victims, might have done all this, yes, for she was that good, that fine, that effective a witness for the Lord whom she served with mind, body and soul.

Death came in an instant, death as a thing of steel tore into her frag-ile body, silencing that voice, metamorphosing that trademark smile into something of stone almost, pale, and sightless, taking from her what oth-ers had enjoyed as they came into her presence and experienced the beau-ty of Sydney Browning, the overflowing joy, the invitation to join with her in experiencing the love of Christ Jesus, taking this from her, yes, and leaving nothing in its place but blankness.

Death.

For that perishable body, yes, that it was, death, the heart stopping abruptly, the blood no longer pumping through her veins and arteries as a self-contained recipient of its nourishment but spilling instead out onto the couch where she had been sitting, and splattering the clothes of the others with her, those who proved to be survivors as well as victims like Sydney.

Truly this was death in all its ignominious ferocity, in all its ugli-ness and grisliness and whatever else, death closing the door of life. But that body was not Sydney Browning, just the veneer, the surface, the form wrapped around that which was really this 36-year-old champion of righteousness.

Sydney Browning was not dead; she was released, a spirit now like the angel Darien who greeted her as she looked at him in awe.

"You are so beautiful," she spoke.

"Not I, dear child of the King," he replied, "for I am as discarded potter's clay compared to you. I was created to serve you. And I am here now to bring you into the presence of your Savior."

She would have cried then if she could but tears were gone forever, tears belonged to flesh, tears banished as was sorrow, as was pain.

She saw her body.

"Angel?" she asked.

"Yes?" Darien responded.

"Am I truly...?"

Words failed, as words often did for those who no longer saw through a glass darkly.

"Yes, Sydney, you as you once were, are no longer. You as your Cre-ator meant you to be, are."

She examined herself.

"I am so much like you," she observed, her astonishment growing by the fleeing seconds.

"Infinitely more," Darien said, "dear, dear one. God has focused His entire plan for the ages around you and many, many more like you. On this the whole of human history has been written."

She saw others ascending from that sanctuary, an angel with each, Cassie, Kim, Kristie, Joey, Mary Beth and Shawn.

Slowly, in awe ever, Sydney glanced upward.

"I see..." she started to say, the lights of Heaven beaming so brightly, yet she did not have to turn away.

"Yes, you do, and He is—"

Sydney gasped because after years of witnessing for Him, after hours spent in soul-deep prayer, after awaiting that moment, though never suspecting that it would come as soon as it had, she saw Jesus smiling, not in her mind's eye, not through pages of Scripture, not in quiet times of draining from her consciousness everything and everyone except Him; she saw in the blessed reality of that instant, she saw Him truly, saw Him as He was, saw Him turn toward her.

And reach out His hands to her, to the six others.

"So much love from Him..." Sydney said, trying to deal with the wonder of what was happening. "And that love is touching me right now, wrapping around me like a warm blanket on a cold winter's morning."

Countless numbers had struggled with the need to express themselves, in words halting or eloquent.

"Eternally, Sydney," angel Darien assured her. "You will know nothing else...ever again."

Singing.

Familiar.

Words with which she herself had blessed others from a hymn that was the song of her very life.

"To a home on God's celestial shore...."

And then she soared, with the angel at her side, soared through time and space, and beyond.

"To a land where joys shall never end...."

Ten thousand upon ten thousand angels were joining in the chorus, the words now a part of her liberated soul.

"When I die, hallelujah..."

She looked back but once, looked below at the confusion in that sanctuary, at the pain on the faces of the wounded, the pain of loved ones left behind, the fear and the confusion...and she heard the cries of the very young, their place of peace rent asunder by an intruding stranger.

And she turned toward the glory of the One for whom she had been willing to give up her earthly life.

"Welcome, good and faithful servant," her Savior, her Lord spoke. "I give you rest, Sydney Browning."

"Yes, Lord, oh, my precious, precious Lord...praise Your holy name."

"You have," He told her simply. "You have done just that."

And Sydney Browning entered triumphantly into a wholly new reality beyond the corrosive reach of the old, the legendary golden streets spreading without end before her as creatures of transcendent beauty bid her welcome.

Chapter 13

Shawn Brown had been actively preparing himself for entry into heaven for a very long time prior to the death of his finite existence, studying in depth what the biblical passages had to say and talking at length with top theologians at Southwestern Baptist Theological Seminary about a variety of subjects, Heaven being one of these. And there were the many, many books he had sought from insightful recommendations by faculty members including Berry Driver, the exceptionally gifted dean of libraries, a man of great wisdom whose services were invaluable to SWBTS.

"Heaven will be my eventual home," he said more than once, "but I am prepared to live fully in *this* life as well."

Shawn could have been, by any accounts, the hero of the evening. His natural impulse, given his football-hero size, would have been to sneak up on thin, almost emaciated-looking Larry Ashbrook, and, in short order, overpower the intruder, and there would have been no hint of self-aggrandizement, his only consideration the safety of young people he had come to know and love.

Shawn did have such a chance, a chance to complete what some observers said was undoubtedly in his mind.

As soon as Ashbrook noticed him, perceiving him as a genuine threat, a burly young man who could thwart his violent desires, the trigger of the gun in his hand was pulled more than once, bullets finding their target, tossing his adversary to the floor, and sending bursts of blood in several directions.

Shawn, as the others being sent from a familiar finite world into one where death is banished, would die in an instant.

Pain.

A momentary surge of pain like no other that he had ever before felt hit him broadside as he was being knocked off his feet, slamming the floor hard.

And then—

"Oh, Lord, Lord..." Shawn whispered, trembling, as angel Stedfast stood before him.

"No, young man, it is not He," the other said. "I am here to take you to your Lord."

Shawn looked at the other rising souls. He saw Kim and Sydney and—

"She seems to be singing," Stedfast remarked.

"She was always like that," Shawn noted.

"For her, it will be no different in that respect, except that she will feel like singing every moment."

"Moment?"

"Just a manner of speaking."

"There is no time recognized in heaven, is there?"

"No time for time," Stedfast offered.

The young man then spoke of his wife.

"Kathy Jo will have it so rough," Shawn spoke up, as her image crossed his mind, and he understood the anguish she would feel when she learned of what had happened to him.

"And so will the loved ones of six other young people," Stedfast reminded him. "It will be a form of hell for them over the coming months."

"Can't I—?"

The angel interrupted, knowing what great masses of people had said over the many centuries since the first death of a human being, reactions very much the same, one after the other, throughout history

"No need," Stedfast spoke. "She will join you eventually."

For the briefest moment, Shawn was gripped by the last lingering gasp of earthly sorrow.

"How long?" he asked.

"Years."

"How can I wait?"

"In heaven it will be but an instant."

Shawn brightened as he said, "I remember! Praise God I remember about the difference."

"Are you ready now?" asked Stedfast.

"No more kids to bring to Christ..." he muttered. "How strange that really will seem."

"Think of your legacy."

"My legacy?"

"The numbers for whom you already have been an instrument of conversion...they will bend their knees and in prayer thank you for being what you were, prayer that will rise up to the throne of God Himself."

"After a few years, they'll still remember, still care?"

"For the rest of their lives."

Shawn as spirit felt more deeply, saw more clearly.

"I remember a sad young man," he recalled just then, "a young man who felt so alone that he wanted to die."

"He will be at the memorial service, Shawn, and he will stand up, tears flowing down his cheeks, as he raises his hands toward heaven, and he will tell everyone what you did for him. Someday, he will get married, and his wife and he will teach their children what you taught him."

"Oh my...."

"Yes, wonderful, is it not?"

"Angel?"

"Yes?" *Stedfast asked, anticipating from millennia of experience what this bright young soul was going to say.*

"I'm ready."

"*I know, Shawn, I know.*"

He ascended with Stedfast and the other martyrs, passed the blazing-bright gates of heaven along with them, and found himself met by redeemed souls whose flesh-and-blood forms had died before his own, whether weeks or months or years before, it did not matter, waiting for him they were, and they would tell him of their love, love for the young man who took them in his arms, and shared their pain, their sorrow, their despair, and, now, through the grace of God, their salvation as well.

Chapter 14

Darien and Stedfast returned to the sanctuary in what finite terms might be called an instant....

The crescendo of terror was increasing.

Initially, those attending the rally who sat in the front pews were not aware of what was going on.

"We all thought some sort of skit was being played," one of them commented later.

But in seconds the truth hit them in two different ways.

According to one report, a teenager sitting in one of the middle pews tried to shift her legs but her feet seemed mired in some sticky substance like gum, but red along with specks of gray.

Not gum.

The bomb was next.

Larry Ashbrook threw his homemade weapon of terror, and it exploded upward but not outward, away from hundreds of helpless young people, the targets of his madness protected somehow.

For Darien and Stedfast, there was no doubt about what happened; no "somehow" at all.

"Look!" Darien spoke.

Other angels, a double row of them standing at the front of the sanctuary, creatures of iridescence forming a solid wall of light.

"Our comrades!" Stedfast exclaimed, though not really surprised over the sight directly ahead.

Later, many of those present would report impressions of light, pinpoints of it flashing briefly in front of the podium.

Stedfast turned and looked to one side.

Fallen angels were screeching.

"They have failed hundreds of times this night, so many souls beyond their malignant grasp," Darien remarked as he, too, noticed their foul hordes. "And they are in a hellish frenzy."

Protection, yes, for the great majority of those in attendance that night but not for another victim.

Kim Jones.

He fired.

In the same row, two seconds later, two young women shielded a retarded teenager. One was shot in the back but because she had severe curvature of the spine, the bullet was deflected and did comparatively little harm.

That same moment, Kim's breathing stopped, and she closed her eyes for the final time of her too-few years. On her face was an expression not of complete terror but, rather, of overriding peace.

Kim stood just inside the entrance to a kingdom in which she had believed fervently.

"I never had any doubt," she told Darien just before he left her to return yet again to Wedgwood Baptist Church. "I believed and doubt fled. For three years I felt His presence."

She was silent briefly, then asked, "My mother, my father, my brother...I know how this is going to affect them."

"Great sorrow," the angel remarked honestly. "All three will know great sorrow."

"I wish I could comfort them."

That was Kim's only concern then, the welfare of others, which had been typical of her.

"You will," Darien assured her.

"But how?"

"By the memories they have of you."

She wanted to cry but as with the others, no longer could, as promised by Scripture.

"I wish there was more than just that."

"Your journal, Kim."

"It contained just a few ramblings," she said, ever modest.

"No, it was more than that. Your journal gives those who love you the most intimate of your thoughts. Your mother will find it and read every line over and over. It will tell your parents and your brother a great deal, but especially the joy that is present page after page."

Darien paused, then went on to add, "For your mother especially, those entries will be her lifeblood in a sense, nourishing her as memories return on cold, lonely nights."

It was time to go.

"Kim?" Darien asked.

"Do you recall that woman you were able to bring to the Lord just two days before she died?"

Kim thought briefly, and suddenly brightened, her radiance exceeding that of the angel.

"Yes, yes!" she replied, "I do!"

"She is so eager to thank you."

"I was happy for her. I really felt good because she had had such a rough, sad life, and, in a short while, all that would change."

"See for yourself, sweet child."

Two figures: the same woman no longer pale, frightened but radiant, standing at the side of Jesus Himself.

"My Lord..." whispered the daughter of Stephanie and Stanley Jones.

"My devoted Kim," the Son of God replied. "We have been waiting, this precious soul and I."

And then, freed of finite fleshly bondage, Kim Jones stepped into the glory of that place everlasting.

Part III

Is death the last sleep? No, it is the last and final awakening.
Sir Walter Scott

Chapter 15

...dancing in God's playground.

That was a striking comment made later by a key faculty member at Southwestern Baptist Theological Seminary, a statement carrying with it the urgency of unequivocal truth.

Or what Francis Schaeffer called "true truth."

...God's playground.

Normally thought a sanctuary, the safest of places.

No longer.

Due to yet another abhorrent act committed by satan through his fellow fallen, those others who set themselves against God long, long ago.

Else there would never have been the Casting Out, that epochal rending of the loyalties of Heaven's creatures, from total devotion to God for all to a third of their numbers rebelling against deity, and following their ego-dominated leader, Lucifer, into a history-long exile, and a mad attempt to destroy everything and everyone that God would ever create.

Slaughter.

Millions upon millions of men, women and children cruelly dead by sword or spear.

Dead by bullet or bomb blast.

Dead by the strangling hands of intruders.

Dead by a hundred different means, many sent to Heaven but hosts more off to the environs of a receptive hell.

And there were others, babies sacrificed before birth to the madness of abortion, one of satan's favorite tools, a tool that had claimed tens of millions of lives during just the second half of the twentieth century.

Blood on the taloned hands of the creature who originated evil.

Suddenly, satan had invaded the physical conditions of a church, through a human surrogate.

And his demons were dancing frenziedly in that once secure playground now a place of death.

The sight seemed out of hell itself.

The most loathsome creatures were skittering down the aisles of Wedgwood Baptist Church, Fort Worth, Texas.

Foul beings whose source of greatest pleasure was inflicting the most anguish upon God's creations, from the very young to the aged.

But, mostly, that night of September 15, 1999, it was the young whom his minions hoped to grab and drag off to damnation.

"But this is a church!" one of the lesser horde exclaimed. "What can we accomplish here?"

"Our kind? In churches?" another spoke. "Where have you been? We do it all the time through false doctrines/heresies, through sexual aberration, through the appeal to wealth, through all this and far more."

Nupain approached them.

Overjoyed.

He saw the others looking at him.

"It is so grand," he said, his manner jubilant. "That poor fool just killed someone else."

"Who was that?" one of the creatures asked, an underlying concern readily apparent.

"Long-haired type...Steggy Ray," Nupain replied coldly, his contempt unconcealed.

The other demon turned away.

"What bothers you?" Nupain inquired.

"I think...."

"You think what?"

"I heard him talking about his plans for the future just before our stooge entered the building."

"Plans? So what?"

"He was a fine young man."

"You could say that about any of our male victims. The finer they are, the greater the victory for our kind."

"But this one especially...this Steggy Ray...he had potential... though he might not give that impression on first glance."

"I am quite sure he did, potential for righteousness. Remember that? Such potential we do not need!"

"But now he is gone from this world."

"A victory, is it not? For our kind!"

"Our kind? Yes, it is such a victory."

"But your regret is obvious. Think of the grief he could have caused us if he had not died."

"Nupain?"

"Yes?"

"I was by his side when it happened."

"My oh my, some demons have all the luck!" Nupain remarked in a celebratory mood.

"He saw me, and he smiled."

"Steggy Ray smiled?"

"Oh, he did, a grand smile."

"As he was looking at you, of all things. As you once were, while still in Heaven, yes, I could imagine that. But look at you now. You are as ghastly as the rest of us. And yet he smiled at you?"

"That was what I thought at first. But then I realized that he did not see me at all. He...he was looking right through me, Nupain, as though I was not even here, as though I mattered not the slightest."

Nupain said nothing, all too familiar with what manifold numbers of fellow fallen angels had told him again and again over the millennia that had passed since the Casting Out occurred but, still, for a short while, he needed to keep up a front, however false it was.

And so he feigned ignorance.

"Go ahead," he nudged. "Tell me more."

"Nupain, he saw instead Darien," the demon added. "I was as dirt under his feet. He was smiling at our former comrade."

If this creature, so grotesque as he was, could have cried, then tears would be flowing then and there.

"I stepped aside as Darien went past. He looked at me, and there was an invitation in his manner."

"Invitation?" Nupain said. "To forsake us, to rejoin him and the rest of his brethren?"

"Yes...."

"What a fantasy, do you not agree?"

A demon casting his master aside? The very thought caused sneers to ripple through that crowd, their disbelief reeking.

Hurriedly, lest the wrong impression be sustained, that very same demon spoke again, with a lack of conviction that seemed to go right past the normally alert Nupain.

"A fantasy, yes..." he told them all, "that's what it is...nothing more."

Chapter 16

There was more than demonic activity at Wedgwood Baptist Church on September 15, 1999.

Light.

Witnesses reported seeing flashes of light, not reflections from church lighting but something else, quite different, light of great intensity but near-split second brevity, seen once then gone.

And something else.

A force for righteousness that spotted Larry Ashbrook in his tracks, that sent the unseen demonic forces reeling.

Teenager Jeremiah Neitz.

He had come to Christ three months earlier, in the midst of a very troubled period in his life.

And now, suddenly, he stood, and approached Ashbrook face to face.

A second passed, no more.

Jeremiah bravely claimed the name of his Savior, and pleaded with the intruder to stop.

Those inside who were fallen angels went into a frenzied panic.
"There are more who must die!" they screamed. "Not enough blood has been shed. We need to be filled up with more anguish."

Nupain personally stood beside Ashbrook, filling his mind with hate, urging him on, and on, and on.

And there was the teenager, knowing nothing about what was going on in the realm of spiritual warfare that had gripped the sanctuary, there was Jeremiah, his face pleading as much as his words, but no real fear, no sense of flinching, no last minute desire to turn and run.

Just simple words.

"Stop in the name of Jesus!" he uttered.

One young man among hundreds of other young people.

The demonic army arrayed against him could not compete with his faith, a babe in Christ vanquishing the shrieking, bloodthirsty hordes from hell that could not be seen but their fury felt.

Larry Ashbrook sat down and shot himself.

Just one bullet.

Dozens of lives could have been next. But the courage of one teenage boy ended the slaughter.

That night the veil between the finite and the infinite, between flesh and blood and the supernatural was rent.

In the blinking of an eye only, but rent just the same, unfallen angels protecting hundreds of young lives against an onrush of hordes of damned fallen ones, creatures once glorious now far more ghastly than the most gruesome monsters in the most graphic horror films made by perverse human minds.

A battle.

Demons prowling the aisles of Wedgwood Baptist, seeking those whom they might destroy, ravenous beasts ready to snatch the unsaved from one world into another of endless terror and suffering.

The sight of flowing blood drove them to ever greater frenzy, cries of pain from the dying and the wounded intensifying their frantic pursuit.

And yet, in that place of worship turned slaughterhouse, this horde of the unholy found no one, no souls who had abandoned their Creator, and, therefore, ripe for damnation.

They screamed, they tried mightily to terrorize but they failed en toto, they failed so completely, that each and all dreaded the unnerving report that would have to be presented to their unforgiving master, a creature of encompassing rage once his plans were thwarted.

"No new souls for your domain," they would have to say.

All that satan would achieve for his efforts was the agony of the wounded. But for a creature as perverse as this one, the massive amount of that agony was enough to delight him, though he had hoped to have more, his ultimate design being more souls for hell, not simply the torment of the dying before they were carried off to the heavenly home that once had been his as well.

After Larry Ashbrook committed suicide, unfallen angels Darien and Stedfast watched the demon horde retreat, watched each former comrade hurry off to their present and future home, to their master, to the same damnation that they shared with the lost souls of history.

Both unfallen angels had been told by their Creator that all the wounded would survive, though some would take longer to heal than others because their wounds were more than physical, like David Nix, ten years old at the time, a boy who suffered through months of nightmares.

"There will be more, Stedfast," spoke Darien portentously.

"Shootings," the other angel asked, "bombs?"

"Yes, this evil will spread, at schools across the nation, at supermarkets, at churches."

"Will many be by young people?"

"Indeed, my dear Stedfast, actually by young people as at Columbine, or as at Wedgwood Baptist, by another generation altogether, the barrels of their weapons aimed at the young."

"Satan is on the attack more than ever."

"And he has whole industries aiding him—the producers of violent movies and video games—more than a few with a more dangerous outreach than ever before because of the Internet. Bloody deaths are made entertaining, and there is less and less ability to separate reality from the thrills on theater screens and computer monitors and televisions."

The physically wounded were being taken away, and the emotionally wounded were being initially counseled in a school across the street.

The immediate danger was over.

But there was another.

Young people internalizing their reactions to the nightmare.

"They will be a danger for some time to come," Darien spoke, "either to themselves or to others...more troubled souls out in the world, their behavior unpredictable at any given moment."

"What a victory for satan!" Stedfast exclaimed.

"But, of course, only temporary."

Days later, both angels would attend a memorial service, a service celebrating the survival of the hundreds who did not die, the 99 percent who would continue with their lives.

"The media has been so unusually respectful," Stedfast would say later. "It is as though they have been caught up in the genuine joy that the members of Wedgwood Baptist feel."

"Some of the reporters have admired such resiliency," Darien affirmed. "They wonder how they would react in similar circumstances."

"Darien?"

"Yes, my comrade?"

"Will men, women and children come to know Christ as Savior and Lord because of this?"

"In an uncertain world, in a world torn apart by such violence, with safe harbors fewer and fewer, I cannot see how it could be otherwise. Satan clearly has failed beyond his own worst fears."

"Thank you, dear friend, thank you for that."

And then, as often the case over the many, many centuries, the two were summoned by their Creator to another location where human beings were engaged in spiritual warfare, mortal life ending, as it had done for Sydney Browning, Kim Jones and Shawn Brown, but with all of Heaven waiting for them to pass the gates and experience the embrace of Father, Son and Holy Spirit, an embrace that would never be denied, the enemy of their souls denied victory for forever and ever.

Epilogue

Many of the fallen angels soon fled Wedgwood Baptist Church but not all would leave that general area, for they had been told to form another battle line, one that could yield a rich harvest of human torment.

Plans.

Satan had plans.

He was doing the same thing at Columbine High, torturing the students with anguish so severe that one of them had hung himself in his bedroom; a mother had shot herself to death in a gun shop; and the madness was continuing yet without a predictable end in sight.

"We have accomplished a great deal," he exhorted the mass of creatures before him, though he failed to mention that, out of more than 400 in attendance, only seven were removed, and, yet, even there, he put the best possible "spin" on the circumstances. "Those who died would have given us a terrible time. Because of them, scores of souls were to be lost to us."

The other fallen groaned, as though on cue, knowing what would please their master.

"But the war is not over, obviously," he went on, his tone changing noticeably. "They are going to try and make some kind of victory out of all this."

More groans.

"Yet they have little idea of what we can do with the aftermath," continued satan. *"There is such a thing as post traumatic stress syndrome."*

"That sounds promising," Nupain spoke up.

"It will be, my slave, it will be."

Soon the assembled demons went their separate ways, all except Nupain, who approached his master.

"Such a harvest of misery," he commented with anticipation, *"and it continues on and on."*

Satan was delighted.

"Their ignorance is our exaltation," he said.

"And as you have been saying, since we will ultimately be the victors against God, this business about the lake of fire as our punishment forever and ever is so much nonsense."

Satan turned away just then.

"Master?" asked Nupain. *"That is right, is it not?"*

"I have told you so."

"But, please, all this blood, all these centuries of misery for humankind, we will never be made to pay the price, despite what His prophets have said? They are simply mouthing His lies?"

Satan's silence in response echoed through the flaming corridors of hell and back, like a physical thing, confronting the master of evil with a panorama of the infamy he had inspired through the millennia of time since Eden, while hurting, sorrowing but trustful men, women and children sang hosannas to Almighty God from the sanctuary that was Wedgwood Baptist Church, a sanctuary once and again, their voices reaching heaven itself as angels and the redeemed alike celebrated with joy triumphant, tears and pain and mourning banished like the fallen themselves as they looked up at what once they had, in all its majesty, but never would again.

Living is death; dying is life. On this side of the grave we are exiles; on that, citizens; on this side, orphans; on that side, fresh-faced children filled with awe...on this side, captives; on that, free; on this side, disguised, unknown; on that, disclosed and proclaimed as the sons of God.

Henry Ward Beecher

Afterword

"Where Was God?"

By Kenneth Hemphill

Events such as those at Wedgwood or Columbine always prompt the haunting question, "Where was God?" or the companion query, "Why did God allow such an atrocity?"

During the days following the disaster at Wedgwood, some form of the question about moral evil was the one I was asked to address most frequently.

The secular media seemed to ask the question while pointing a finger of indictment and confusion.

It was as if they were saying, "You folks ought to enjoy some level of protection from such evil since you claim to live your lives for an all-powerful and all-loving God. If what you claim is true, how could your God allow this to happen?"

It was, however, a gentle indictment.

I sensed that the members of the press were deeply moved by the tragedy and were looking for some answers, for a way to make some sense out of an unspeakable act of violence.

It would be unfair and inaccurate to suggest that members of the secular press corps were the only ones asking the question, "Where was God?"

Members of the Christian press corps, our seminary family and Christians across the United States were equally concerned to receive some answers to the moral dilemma raised by the tragic events at Wedgwood.

This was a church gathering.

The youth had gathered to pray for their schools and their country.

The victims were teenagers and young adults. People in the prime of their life. They were Christians! Three of them were either enrolled in the seminary or recent graduates.

In the light of the unusual circumstances, members of the Christian press were pleading for a cogent answer to present to the world.

Questions about life and death, good and evil are a natural part of life, but they are brought into sharper focus by events such as Wedgwood.

In our pain and confusion we cry out for answers.

Why?

Who is to blame?

Where was God?

Can He do anything about evil?

If God is all-powerful and all-loving, then in some way He must be implicated when such events occur.

To argue that God allowed the evil but did not cause it does little, in our minds, to answer the predicament raised by moral and natural evil that brings death and devastation into our lives.

Can We Explain the Presence of Evil?

I find it fascinating that the question about evil is often hurled at Christians in a "somewhat" accusatory manner by the non-Christian asking how a completely good and all-powerful God could permit evil things to happen.

Even people who argue that they do not believe in God are sometimes guilty of accusing Him of causing evil events. They use the presence of evil to confirm their unbelief. They declare that they could never believe in a God who would permit such tragedy and needless suffering.

Such circular reasoning is difficult to understand, but it does challenge us to answer the question posed by the presence of evil.

I think it is never less than relevant and acceptable for the world at large to ask the Christian community if they have any answer for the presence of evil.

Does the Christian faith make sense of our world?

I would remind you that every other worldview must confront and answer this same question. We must ask whether the atheist or the New Age proponent possesses any answers to this question.

I am delighted to tell you that I think Christianity has the only consistent and satisfying answer to the questions of evil and suffering.

There seems to me only three possible solutions to the question of the presence of evil and, alternately, the existence of God. We could argue along with the atheist that evil exists, which thus proves that God does not exist. On the other end of the spectrum we could argue that God certainly exists but also that evil does not exist. This is essentially the view of Hinduism and Christian Science. Between these two extremes lies the view that God and evil both exist. For the sake of completeness and clarity, let's take a brief look at all three options.

1.   God Exists and Evil Does Not Exist.

This view of life argues that God is good and that all evil is an illusion. Readers familiar with the teaching of Christian Science will recognize the teaching of its founder, Mary Baker Eddy. She wrote: "Evil is but an illusion, and it has no real basis."[1] Eddy argued that evil is not real; it is only an error of the mortal mind. Some proponents of New Age thinking have a similar solution to evil since they argue that god is all and all is god. Since god is good, then only good exists.

---

1   Mary Baker Eddy, *Science and Health with Key to the Scriptures* (Boston: Christian Science, 1903), p. 480.

To accept this proposition, we must deny the evidence of our senses and our personal experiences. We must ask, "Why is the illusion of evil so real and so universal?" We see the results of evil, and we experience the suffering it causes.

Are we to disregard all the scientific and historical evidence that points to the real existence of evil, pain and suffering? Would it comfort the families of those killed and wounded at Wedgwood, to tell them that the evil they have experienced is a mere illusion? This suggestion is only wishful thinking and does not provide a valid solution to the problem of evil.

2.   *Evil Exists and God Does Not Exist.*

This answer could be suggested by the atheist because, philosophically, the atheist does not have a problem with evil. For the atheist, evil, death and suffering are guaranteed. The survival of the fittest is inherent in the system of evolution that atheists espouse and therefore a natural part of our earthly existence.

For many atheists, it is the presence of evil that proves God does not exist. If God is all-good and all-powerful, He has a moral obligation to remove evil. Thus the atheist can reason that God does not exist.

Notice first that atheism offers no solution for the problem of evil. It only accepts evil as an inevitable part of the evolutionary process. In truth, it is more difficult for the atheist to account for the presence of good than for the Christian to account for evil. The atheist has no word of comfort to give to the families who lost loved ones at Wedgwood. True atheism is fatalistic and hopeless.

3.   *God Exists and Evil Exists.*

If we deny neither the existence of God or evil, then we must face the resulting tension created by the existence of an all-powerful and all-good God and the presence of evil. Three attempts have been made to resolve this apparent dilemma.

a)   Some have argued that God and evil are opposite and equal. This position is called *dualism*. Those who hold this view accept evil as a real entity that is the opposite of good and that the two have existed together from all eternity.

This idea is represented by the symbol of the yin and the yang that has become popular among many teens. This view may help picture the existence of evil, but it does not help to resolve it.

If both God and evil are coeternal opposites, what hope do we have that God can overcome evil? Dualism is built on false assumptions. It first assumes that the power of evil is equal to the power of God. It also assumes that evil is a "thing" and has an existence of its own.

Evil can better be understood as a corruption of something good that already exists or a privation of that good. Rust, rot and decay are simply the corruption of good things. When evil is not present in a thing, that thing is better. The evil we experienced at Wedgwood was a corruption of the good.

b)   Others have resolved the problem of the coexistence of God and evil by asserting that God exists, but that He lacks the power to control or stop evil. This idea is called *finitism* because it views God as a finite being who struggles with the problem of evil as we do. If evil is to be destroyed, we must join God in the fight.

c)   Some proponents claim they find it easier to relate to a limited God. The view of a finite God who is powerless to resolve evil has been popularized by Rabbi Kushner in his book, *When Bad Things Happen to Good People*. Rabbi Kushner had accepted the traditional Jewish view of God as all-good and all-powerful until the tragic death of his son. Kushner based his conclusions on the Book of Job, stating that a good person like Job did not deserve to experience terrible misfortune.

Why, then, did Job suffer? Kushner concluded, "God wants the righteous to live peaceful, happy lives, but sometimes even He can't bring that about."[2] Kushner claims to find a sense of relief in the discovery that God is limited and therefore not the cause of our misfortunes. He writes, "I can worship a God who hates suffering but cannot eliminate it, more easily that I can worship a God who chooses to make children suffer and die, for whatever exalted reason."[3]

d) Finitism does not offer a satisfactory answer to the question of evil. If God cannot and will not ultimately overcome evil, then we are surely living in a hopeless situation. It also ignores what we do know about God from revelation. It makes God in the image of man rather than man in the image of God.

   If we were to accept this view, we would then have to conclude that Wedgwood is yet another example of God's impotence. What comfort does that bring?

e) Biblical theism argues that God and evil exist but that God is far greater than evil and will ultimately destroy it, meting out its punishment in the lake of fire forever.

   This clearcut biblical response to evil indicates that God has both an immediate as well as long-term solution to the problem of evil.

   We have a message that is both realistic and hopeful. We can and must answer the question posed by events like those which occurred at Wedgwood. We will now turn our attention to a biblical answer.

---

2   Harold S. Kushner, *When Bad Things Happen to Good People* (New York: Schocken Books, 1981), 43.

3   Kushner, *When Bad Things Happen*, 134.

A Biblical Response to the Presence of Evil in the World

I have found it helpful to present the biblical answer to the problem of evil by outlining it in a sequence of steps. Thus, for completeness and simplicity, I will outline a step-by-step answer to the problem of evil.

Step 1. *God's creation is good.*

If we turn our attention to the very first pages of biblical revelation, we find that God created the world and all that is in it from nothing. Repeatedly God declared that His creation was good. For example we might read Genesis 1:31a (NAS): "God saw all that He had made, and behold, it was very good." God's creation was perfect and without sin. God is not the author of evil and cannot tempt man to evil. James 1:13 (NAS) declares: "Let no one say when he is tempted, 'I am being tempted by God'; for God cannot be tempted by evil, and He Himself does not tempt anyone." We can categorically declare that God did not cause the gunman to open fire on the youth gathered at Wedgwood. God is not the author of evil. If God's creation was entirely good, then we must conclude that evil and its resulting misery were a desecration of the good creation of God.

Step 2. *Human beings were created in the image of God, which means they have free will.*

To be created in God's image means that man is relational, rational and responsible.

He is created for relationship with God and man.

He is rational and therefore can understand God's self-revelation. This in turn makes him responsible.

We can see a picture of man's responsibility as God gives Adam and Eve the task of caring for the garden and commands them to avoid the tree of the knowledge of good and evil. We should further note that anything that is created is by definition finite and therefore has the possibility of corruption and non-existence. Every created thing can be distorted and destroyed.

Step 3. *Free choice necessitates the possibility of choosing evil.*
Free choice is itself a good gift of God.

It enables man to freely respond to God's love. But along with the gift comes the possibility of choosing evil. The free choice of mankind was the point at which evil entered God's good creation. Notice that evil was the corruption of a good gift, the gift of free will.

The presence of choice does not necessitate evil, but it allows for the possibility of disobedience and the accompanying evil. If there had not been disobedience, there would not have been a problem with evil. Adam's sin problem has become the problem of mankind at large, because we have all sinned. Paul wrote in Romans 5:12 (NIV), "Just as sin entered the world through one man, and death through sin, and in this way death came to all men, because all sinned."

We can illustrate this from our own experience. A parent permits a child to make choices. That child may make wrong choices, bringing unnecessary evil and suffering on himself and others. The child was not coerced into choosing wrongly. In truth, the parent probably warned him against the wrong choice and indicated the circumstances of such a choice.

We do not blame the parent for the child's choice simply because the parent provided the opportunity to choose. We should not conclude that God caused an evil event simply because He did not prevent it.

Some persons ask why God didn't create the world so that no one could choose evil.

This is simply another way of suggesting that God is responsible for an evil event when He doesn't prohibit such an event. However, we should still answer the question. To do so let's suppose that God created mankind and gave them free will, but prohibited them from choosing evil.

Could we truthfully say that persons are free to choose if they are not able to choose evil? If we visited an ice cream parlor that advertised that we could choose from 32 different flavors but we then discovered that all the flavors were vanilla, we would rightly complain that we were not given a choice.

The opportunity to choose is essential to a moral universe. If God had not given man free will, man would be little more than a robot or a preprogrammed android. As such, man would be incapable of either good or evil. Obedience that is programmed is not really the loving response that God desires from His creation.

Step 4. *The human choice to sin has affected the entire created order.*

Let's read Romans 8:20-22 (NAS): "For the creation was subjected to futility, not willingly, but because of Him who subjected it, in hope that the creation itself also will be set free from its slavery to corruption into the freedom of the glory of the children of God. For we know that the whole creation groans and suffers the pains of childbirth together until now."

Man and the created world are intricately tied together. Man's sin and rebellion have impacted creation in such a way that it groans to be delivered from its slavery to corruption.

In the Genesis story we find that man's sin impacted the bounty of the earth. God had given man all the fruit-bearing plants to provide for his every need. Because of the fall the ground was cursed and Adam's labor became toil because the ground now bore thorns and thistles (see Gen. 3:17-19).

Today we continue to see the impact of sin upon the whole of the created order. We witness the effect of human sin in the pollution and desecration of the environment, which causes human suffering.

Step 5. *Evil cannot be fully understood without recognizing the existence of an evil adversary (see Gen. 3:1-15).*

Satan is the archenemy of man and seeks only to kill, steal and destroy. In John 10 Jesus contrasts His ministry as the Good Shepherd with that of a hireling and a thief who comes only to steal, kill and destroy, while the Good Shepherd comes to give life abundantly (verse 10).

The Bible does not go into great detail about the origin of satan. Apparently, Lucifer, as he was originally named, was created as a beautiful angelic being. Along with other angelic beings, satan chose to rebel against God. Peter mentions satan's rebellion in Second Peter 2:4 (NAS). "For if God did not spare angels when they sinned, but cast them into hell and committed them to pits of darkness, reserved for judgment..." (cf. Jude 6).

The Bible pictures satan as a rebel against God.

He and his angels became the enemies of God and humanity. Satan is the deceiver and the accuser of the human race.

In the Book of Revelation, when we are told of Satan's ultimate defeat, we have a good description of his work. "And the great dragon was thrown down, the serpent of old who is called the devil and satan, who deceives the whole world; he was thrown down to the earth, and his angels were thrown down with him" (12:9 NAS).

Satan tempts man to yield to his fleshly desires and then accuses him of failure, creating unhealthy guilt. We have already looked at James 1:13, which declares that God cannot tempt man to do evil.

Now notice James 1:14-15 (NAS): "But each one is tempted when he is carried away and enticed by his own lust. Then when lust has conceived, it gives birth to sin; and when sin is accomplished, it brings forth death."

If we are looking to assign blame for the Wedgwood tragedy, we need to look to the work of the adversary who tempts man to evil, enticing him to give in to his own sinful desires. It was not God's desire that the gunman takes the lives of the seven Wedgwood martyrs; it was the work of the adversary.

Step 6. *God will totally and finally defeat evil.*

The apostle Paul looked with great anticipation to the final defeat of all evil. He clearly expressed his sure hope in Romans 8:18 (NIV): "I consider that our present sufferings are not worth comparing with the glory that will be revealed in us." When Paul contrasted our present suffering with what was to be our ultimate glory, he concluded that there is no comparison.

The Book of Revelation often speaks of God's final triumph over evil and its personal results. Look, for example at Revelation 21:3-4 (NIV): "I heard a loud voice from the throne saying, 'Now the dwelling of God is with men, and He will live with them. They will be His people, and God Himself will be with them and be their God. He will wipe every tear from their eyes. There will be no more death or mourning or crying or pain, for the old order of things has passed away.' "

Your attention was probably drawn to items such as tears, death, mourning and pain. These four terms describe well the Wedgwood tragedy. Notice that these negative and hurtful things belong to the old order, which is passing away. These things will no longer trouble us when we are with the Lord. God will finally and forever triumph over all evil.

Perhaps you are thinking that all that the Bible offers is a "pie-in-the-sky" answer to our present suffering. In our present tense experience of suffering we should not discount the power of our ultimate hope to bring comfort and healing in the present.

As I had the privilege to minister to the families of our martyrs, they often gave testimony to the strength they received from knowing that their friend or family member was already present with the Lord. The absolute assurance that they would see their loved one again made present suffering more bearable.

Thus our ultimate hope does help bring comfort in the present tense. But we also can affirm that the Bible provides answers about suffering that are present tense. Let's take another step together.

Step 7. *God's gift of free will prevents the present removal of evil.*

To answer the question about God's plan for evil and suffering in the present tense, we must ask again why God simply doesn't destroy all evil now? Although everyone will agree that freedom from evil and suffering in the future will be glorious, we still struggle with the existence of evil in the present.

Usually when we ask about the destruction of evil in the present, we conveniently ignore the evil in our own lives. To remove all sin and the possibility for evil would require that all freedom be eliminated.

Do we want God to remove our free will and program us only to do good? Since freedom is essential to a moral universe, such an action would actually result in a universe that is neither good nor evil.

If God removed our freedom to choose, we would no longer be made in His image. We would no longer have the ability to respond to God's love or to the love of others. Ultimately, if God destroyed all evil, He would annihilate the entire human race, including you and me, since "all have sinned" (Rom. 3:23).

When we ask the question why a good and holy God would tolerate evil, we must look to His incredible patience. The Bible constantly reminds us that God is longsuffering toward us. God so loved His created beings that He does not desire that anyone would be lost (see 2 Pet. 3:9).

Therefore God, who hates evil, endures the existence of evil, in patience, so that all might have the chance to respond to His love and thus to fulfill their created destiny by living in relationship with Him.

When we grieve over the pain and suffering that is caused by evil, we should also think about how much evil must be grieving the heart of the Creator, who made everything ethically, morally and spiritually spotless. It grieves Him to see His creation spoiled and desecrated by the impact of sin.

In Ephesians 4:30 Paul warns the reader that sin grieves the Holy Spirit who seals us unto the day of redemption. Thus we can understand that God does not will evil, but patiently tolerates it with the view that all may come to life in Him.

Step 8. *God ultimately dealt with the problem of evil by sending His own Son to pay the penalty for sin.*

When we take Romans 3:23 and Romans 6:23 together, we are able to see the incredible problem that sin creates for mankind.

One declares that "all have sinned," and the other indicates that "the wages of sin is death."

All of us deserve the wages of sin.

Yet God in His mercy sent His own Son in human flesh. Jesus was a man in every sense of the word, but He lived without sin. He died on a Roman cross to pay the penalty for our sin and rebellion.

The Bible uses several images to declare this incredible truth. In Second Corinthians 5:21 (NIV) we read: "God made Him who had no sin to be sin for us, so that in Him we might become the righteousness of God."

Peter states it in this manner: "For Christ also died for sins once for all, the just for the unjust, so that He might bring us to God" (1 Pet. 3:18a NAS). Paul, in Colossians 1:20, speaks of God reconciling all things to Himself by Christ's blood on the cross. Christ's blood refers to His death.

A popular song speaks of our owing a debt we could not pay and Christ paying a debt He did not owe. This truth has been illustrated in several different ways, but let me share one of my favorites.

Two college friends who had not seen each other in years met one day in a courtroom. One was the judge and the other the defendant. As the trial progressed, it became apparent that the accused was guilty as charged.

The accused thought that the judge would let him go free because of their friendship. When the time came for the verdict to be announced, he was shocked because the judge declared him guilty and set a stiff fine for the crime.

After sentencing him, the judge removed his robe, stepped from behind the desk and voluntarily paid his friend's fine, thus by that single action satisfying the requirement of the law.

The judge's sense of justice required that he pass the sentence appropriate to the crime; his grace and mercy prompted him to pay the penalty.

That is precisely what God did for us when He sent His Son to pay the penalty of our sin.

May I ask you, the reader, a personal question? Do you know for certain that you have eternal life? I'm not asking you if you are a religious person or a church member. Have you admitted your sinfulness and accepted Christ as the payment for your sin by inviting Him to come into your heart and to be your Lord and Savior? If not, why not do so right now?

Step 9. *When evil brings human suffering, God cares, promises His presence and promises to bring good from evil.*

Although we will consider personal suffering later, for now we will examine a Bible promise that can sustain us through every circumstance of life: "We know that in all things God works for the good of those who love Him, who have been called according to His purpose" (Rom. 8:28 NIV).

This verse does not say that everything is good. It does not say that God causes evil or uses evil to accomplish His will. God would not use that which is contrary to His stated will to accomplish His will.

God did not put it in the heart of the killer to walk into Wedgwood on that fateful night. That action came from Ashbrook's own evil intention as he yielded himself to the work of the adversary.

Yet Romans 8 does assure us that God can work through every circumstance to bring good to those who love Him. God's purpose is not thwarted by evil. God is so powerful that the work of the adversary and the disobedience of man cannot thwart His ultimate purpose.

In the days, weeks and months following the Wedgwood tragedy, we saw God work good from evil.

We saw a new level of commitment among our students.

We saw many young people come to know Jesus Christ through the testimony of the Wedgwood survivors. We have experienced God's peace and comfort.

We have experienced His promise to conform us to the image of His Son (see Rom. 8:29).

Where Is God in Our Suffering?

The Wedgwood Baptist Church tragedy has caused immense human suffering. The families and friends of those who were killed are still enduring the pain that comes from loss. The young people who were wounded by the random shots of the gunman are still suffering the impact of those wounds.

People who were present when the shootings occurred are still struggling with deep emotional and psychological scars. Some are having flashbacks and horrifying nightmares.

The routine of their lives has been disrupted. In some sense all of us are suffering as a result of the Wedgwood tragedy. We have lost our innocence and our sense of security.

If you are not safe at church or at school, where are you safe?

The question of suffering is an issue separate from evil, but it is a related one. It is often tied to the problem of evil with questions such as:

Why do bad things happen to good people?

What does God have against me?

What did I do to deserve this?

Why do we suffer?

Where is God when we suffer?

These are valid and practical questions for which the Bible alone provides satisfactory answers. Let's pose and answer two questions.

Why do we suffer?

Where is God when we suffer?

Why do we suffer?

Although it seems obvious in the case of Wedgwood that our suffering was caused by the evil actions of the gunman, other events that cause suffering are not as easily understood. For that reason it may be helpful to look at several reasons that we may suffer.

1.   *Suffering results from the evil and bad decisions of others.*

A gunman walks into a sanctuary and opens fire. A drunk driver loses control and hits another car. A father abuses his daughter. The laziness of parents creates a financial situation that inflicts suffering on the entire family. These sinful actions and bad decisions of others may cause innocent people to suffer. Here again we must remember that if God were to eliminate free will, He would eliminate our opportunity to know and experience Him, which is our very reason for being.

2. *Suffering results from the fallen state of creation.*

Paul wrote: "The creation itself will be liberated from its bondage to decay and brought into the glorious freedom of the children of God" (Rom. 8:21 NIV).

When sin entered the world, it profoundly affected the entire created order. After the fall in the garden, Adam was told that the once-fruitful ground had been cursed so that it would bear thorns and thistles (see Gen. 3:18). The woman is told that she would have increased pain in childbirth (see Gen. 3:16).

What was then true of the human family continues to be true of the entire created order. Genetic defects and natural catastrophes are both possibilities and realities because of the impact of sin. Thus our suffering can be the result of the fallen state of creation.

3. *Suffering results from our bad choices.*

Suffering is often inherent in the choices we make. For example, the smoker risks cancer; the user of alcohol may develop cirrhosis of the liver; and the overeater may find that the extra weight affects physical well-being. Someone who commits sexual sin risks serious disease, unwanted pregnancy and deep psychological scarring.

An angry God does not cause these results that produce suffering. The risks are inherent in the bad decisions.

This is what Paul meant in Romans 1:27 when he declared that those committing indecent and disobedient sexual acts would receive the due penalty of the error in their own flesh. The sinful act opens the individual to the inherent consequences of the act. God's laws are designed to protect us from unnecessary suffering, but when we choose to violate them we often suffer. This is why obedience to God's Word is so important to abundant living.

4. *Suffering results from the work of the adversary.*

The Bible tells us that satan desires to kill, steal and destroy. The Gadarene demoniacs described in Matthew 8 were suffering because of the activity of a demon. Job's suffering was directly related to the work of the adversary. We also should realize that satanic activity may relate to our sinful choices.

5. *Suffering results from the operation of natural laws.*

The rain that brings the harvest also can bring devastating floods. A hurricane or earthquake can bring pain and suffering. These natural disasters also may be related to the impact of sin on the created order.

6. *Suffering can be for the sake of righteousness.*

Jesus is the perfect example of a righteous person who suffered at the hands of evildoers.

You may lose a job because you report a colleague for stealing. That righteous act brought undeserved suffering. When you suffer for righteousness, remember Jesus' words of encouragement: "Blessed are those who are persecuted because of righteousness, for theirs is the kingdom of heaven" (Matt. 5:10 NIV).

7. *Suffering is sometimes a mystery.*

We desire to be perfect in our understanding, but we do not always clearly understand everything that happens in life. Why are some children born with physical defects? We may offer suggestions, but we can not always give definitive answers.

Where is God when we suffer?
This is the question that hits at the heart of our human situation.

When we suffer, does God really care?

Can He do anything to help us to overcome our suffering?

According to a humanistic worldview, we must accept suffering as inevitable. A proponent of New Age thinking sees suffering as wrong thinking or as the results of actions in a previous life (the law of karma).

The Bible alone provides helpful answers. Carefully read Romans 8:26-28 (NIV): "the Spirit helps us in our weakness. We do not know what we ought to pray for, but the Spirit Himself intercedes for us with groans that words cannot express. And He who searches our hearts knows the mind of the Spirit, because the Spirit intercedes for the saints in accordance with God's will. And we know that in all things God works for the good of those who love Him, who have been called according to His purpose."

This passage suggests four ways that God participates in our suffering:

1. **God helps us in our weaknesses.**

    God is not aloof from our suffering. He grieves with us as a parent would grieve over a wounded child. God not only grieves with us, but He also gives us strength to endure.

    Note what Paul declares in First Corinthians 10:13 (NIV): "...God is faithful; He will not let you be tempted beyond what you can bear. But when you are tempted, He will also provide a way out so that you can stand up under it." God gives us supernatural strength to endure the suffering. I often heard survivors of Wedgwood say, "If not for God's strength, I couldn't have endured."

2. **God gives us the Spirit to intercede for us.**

    Sometimes in our suffering we are at a loss for words and truly do not know how to pray. But God has not left us alone; He has sent the Holy Spirit to intercede for us.

    When I arrived at Wedgwood Baptist Church soon after the shooting, I walked the hallways of the school where the students had been gathered awaiting the arrival of the parents. I heard students praying, weeping and singing.

As I listened, I noticed that sobbing would frequently be interrupted by the sound of praise songs. I knew that I was witnessing the work of the Spirit as He interpreted the inarticulate prayers of the students.

3. **God works in everything for our good.**
    Romans 8:28 does not say that God causes all things. God cannot cause evil. God does not cause that which is contrary to His stated will in order to accomplish His will. The verse does say that God works redemptively in and through all things. Remember that God's understanding is perfect and that our understanding of the good may differ from His.

    God's desire is to make us like His Son. This is the point at which we are called to test the strength of our faith.

    Do we believe that the highest aim in life is to please our Creator and to live in perfect relationship with Him?

    Or do we think that the goal of life is to be happy, comfortable and free of pain? Sometimes our goal of comfort and God's desire for our glorification may collide. You might ask, "How does God work for my good even in suffering?" Let me offer a few suggestions:

    He grows us into the image of His only begotten Son.

    All of Scripture affirms the truth that if we are to be like Christ in His glory, we must join Him in His suffering.

    In Philippians 3:10-11, Paul tells us that he prayed that he might know the fellowship of His sufferings so that he might attain to the resurrection from the dead.

    In Romans 5:3-5 (NIV) Paul explained how suffering and tribulation could lead to spiritual growth. "...We also rejoice in our sufferings, because we know that suffering produces perseverance; perseverance, character; and character, hope. And hope does not disappoint us, because God has poured out His love into our hearts by the Holy Spirit, whom He has given us." In our antiseptic and sedated culture, we want growth without pain.

Suffering often provides a point of revelation.
Suffering sometimes enables us to understand more of God's purpose for our lives.

Hosea, an Old Testament prophet, gained new insight through the suffering caused by an unfaithful wife. Paul also testified to this reality in Second Corinthians 12:8-9.

He prayed that God would remove his thorn in the flesh. The thorn was not removed, but Paul came to a deeper understanding of the sufficiency of God's grace.

Suffering can bring out the best in people. The story of Joni Eareckson Tada has become well known. A quadriplegic, she is an accomplished artist, author and speaker. When we allow God to work with us for good, suffering can be a point of revelation.

Suffering often keeps us from greater evil.
As you read the Old Testament, you will frequently see occasions when suffering kept Israel from greater evil. For example, Joseph suffered separation from his family so that Israel would not have to suffer the ravages of famine. I've seen immediate suffering save some of our singles from disastrous marriage.

An individual experienced great pain when a meaningful relationship was broken by the other person. Yet as time progressed and they saw the unfolding of the other person's character, the injured party praised God that the small pain prevented greater injury.

Suffering is part of the probationary period of life.
As believers, we already have been assured of our eternal citizenship in Heaven, where we will have perfect,

unhindered fellowship with the Father. Peter speaks of this as a probationary period. "In this you greatly rejoice, though now for a little while you may have had to suffer grief in all kinds of trials. These have come so that your faith—of greater worth than gold, which perishes even though refined by fire—may be proved genuine and may result in praise, glory and honor when Jesus Christ is revealed" (1 Pet. 1:6-7 NIV).

If we could avoid all suffering, we would relinquish opportunities to develop more mature faith.

Suffering often provides a platform for witnessing.
Heroic faith through suffering gives a powerful testimony to God's power to sustain His children.

Corrie ten Boom, a seemingly obscure woman, has touched the lives of countless millions by sharing her testimony of God's provision during her imprisonment in Hitler's reign.

Joseph suffered because of his brothers' evil decision, and yet he was given an exceptional opportunity to witness to God's sovereignty in a pagan nation.

It would be difficult to assess the incredible number of opportunities that survivors of Wedgwood have had to bear strong testimony to the goodness of God.

We all have heard of numerous persons who have come to a saving faith in Jesus Christ because of the deaths of the martyrs and the witness of the survivors.

Suffering can often bring us into a closer fellowship with God who suffers with us.
God has already paid the supreme price to relieve suffering permanently by sending His only begotten Son, who voluntarily suffered the penalty of our sin.

If He loved us this much, we can know that He is willing to participate in our suffering.

4.   **God promises that nothing can separate us from Him (Rom. 8:35-39).**
Paul looked at the intense suffering caused by persecution, famine and peril and concluded that in all these things we are more than conquerors because we know that none of these can separate us from God's love.

Because God in His mercy does not desire to destroy humankind, evil still remains. Suffering is real and it causes pain. When you experience suffering, *please* ask yourself, "What would be the worst thing that could happen to me in my present suffering?"

You could lose your job, your family, your health or even your life. But if you have a personal relationship with God through His Son, you can never lose that relationship.

One day there will be no more suffering and pain.

Until then you as a Christian can rest assured that nothing, absolutely nothing, can separate you from God's love in Christ Jesus.

Appendix

"The Devil Was Doing a Dance in God's Playground"

Dr. Ian Jones

Interviewed by
Roger Elwood

The devil was doing a dance in God's playground....

That was how Dr. Ian Jones characterized the rampage at Wedgwood Baptist Church by Larry Ashbrook. Although he is a man who generally takes a conservative position regarding psychological causes of imbalance versus demonization of an individual, he seemed not at all equivocal when the subject was Ashbrook.

"Even, as a professional, when I look at the mental issue, I have to ask what in the world is going on here?" he remarked recently to a journalist. "He trashed a house before he passed several other churches and finally stopped at Wedgwood, which, after all, is hardly the most accessible...in a residential neighborhood not close to a main thoroughfare.

"Behavior this extreme is not just a manifestation of chemical imbalance in the brain. The devil was, I believe, doing a dance in God's playground the night of September 15, 1999."

He leaned back in a chair next to his desk in an office where every available inch was taken up with books.

"This is a nation that generally provides safety and security for churches," Dr. Jones continued. "The medieval concept of the church is as an absolute sanctuary safe from all civil and/or military intrusion."

He grimaced as he recalled images common to Christians in certain other countries around the world.

"It's different elsewhere, in many other places. In East European countries, for example, before the downfall of Communism, churches could be invaded with impunity at any given moment.

"It was also clearly this way in Nazi Germany with those churches that did not practice collaboration with the Gestapo. And the list of congregations facing intimidation, and worse, grows as one thinks of Idi Amin and other dictators in Africa, South America and a long list of additional places.

"Over the years, it has been risky to attend church in more than one European or Asian country. Look at Cuba even today. There, for example, any moment, the doors could be burst open and people storm in with guns. And China is engaging in a renewed crackdown on Christians.

"But here, in the United States, the contrast is striking. This is not to say that shootings in churches have been greeted in almost a cavalier fashion elsewhere. But I can tell you that the Wedgwood tragedy is far more shocking here because it is so completely unprecedented."

Dr. Jones closed his eyes for a moment as he recalled counseling with dozens of young people who attended the September 15, 1999, service.

"Their whole sense of security has gone through a kind of emotional earthquake," he spoke. "They have to start from scratch, many of them."

He smiled hopefully, adding, "More than a year later, some are still working through but, generally, they give hope that they are going to be okay. Others are struggling, really struggling."

"What a fine man!" Stedfast exclaimed.

"Cares a great deal," offered Darien. "So many people in his profession become desensitized after years of counseling. Their own emotions are worn down, and they end up only going through the motions."

Ian Jones had escaped that trap because the love Jesus had for him and other Christians kept his own sensitivity fresh, vibrant.

"Not that he avoids being tired," Darien continued. "Every man, every woman who works as he does needs replenishing from time to time."

"Darien?" asked Stedfast.

"Yes, my comrade."

"We never seem to wear down, as you say, do we?"

"That is very true though, as you know, we come close sometimes, perilously close."

"I think—"

"Go ahead, express what it is that you are thinking."

"Because we are so closely linked with our Creator."

"Whereas human beings are separated from Him by sin, which is, after all, what sin means...being separated from God."

"That is it, dear friend."

And the two would continue to think about that until their next assignment, waiting as they anticipated the direction of the One who gave them their very existence.

Author's Confession

Prayer is not overcoming God's reluctance;
It is laying hold of His highest willingness.
Richard Trench

Author's Confession

I have to spell out more completely what I alluded to earlier, that from virtually the moment I commenced writing this latest of my *Angelwalk* books, I began to experience perhaps the most severe demonic intrusion of my life.

Perhaps?

No...actually it was the *worst*, without equivocation, as I look back on those days from about April onward last year, a time of the severest depression, the breaking up of relationships—some quite new, others spanning the decades—and near-death auto-involved accidents.

Think about this:

I came to Southwestern Baptist Theological Seminary thinking that I was going to stay for the rest of my life.

As I write this, I am instead preparing to *leave* barely a year later, relationships in disarray, the dream turned into a pathetic and rather unsettling nightmare.

Demonic possession is not the same as demon oppression.

Unger makes that clear.

But he also hints that the latter can be so pervasive that the differences almost do not matter.

Just three months after arriving, I got a hint of things to come when my car—a brand-new luxury SUV—was parked in a dean's driveway, and suddenly started backing down into the street.

Then, down the street, driving me part of the way!

Mysteriously, it changed course, backed into a neighbor's driveway, and smashed up against a stone wall.

Another time, the brakes failed in traffic.

And there were other instances with this car.

Purely a run-of-the-mill lemon, like countless others? Or the beginning of a demonic onslaught?

Listen to what the dean told me afterwards:

"Roger, it was as though an unseen hand had reached into that car of yours and turned the wheel so it ended up where it did, rather than in somebody's living room, or hitting a child who happened to be running across the street. I have never seen anything like what happened!"

When made aware of what happened, the dealer disclaimed any responsibility. And they reported *me* to SWBTS!

I know this: It was real, and disturbing. And only Christian faith got me through it all.

...through it all.

A great deal else happened.

There were those evenings when strange noises permeated the immediate area where my house was located.

Shrieking....

I have had cats for nearly 50 years, and I have never heard sounds of such chilling intensity.

Other sounds.

Like someone walking through the house, and yet no one could be found. (Our cats awoke from a sound sleep to listen!)

And my moods.

Dark, depressed...day after day...unrelenting in their savage impact upon my state of mind.

Severe head pains in the middle of the night, stroke-like, in fact, causing me to sob in agony.

And more, so much more.

Before I started this book, everything seemed bright, happy, promising the kind of future I coveted. I would sit on the front porch, and I would look up at the sky, thank God for His grace, His kindness.

Within a week afterwards, all that was changing.

John Babler had warned me early on, and now his words seemed completely prophetic.

The immediate past is littered with the pitiable remains of numerous ruptured relationships, as well as the emotional carnage wrought by rampant ill will, and aborted plans, to be sure, special plans, extraordinary plans that offered exciting opportunities geared to benefit significantly the Cause of Christ.

Gone forever.

Wait a minute now!

Am I saying that satan won this time, our enemy now wallowing in his nefarious triumph?

No.

He did not.

Our adversary lost badly.

What proof is there that he did?

You've just read it.

We are always in the forge, or on the anvil; by trials God is shaping us for higher things.

Henry Ward Beecher

Excerpts From
The Angel and the Judgment
by Don Nori

When the light was gone, so was the angel. Out of the darkness and silence that followed loomed an eerie sense that something had just happened in the heavens and was about to visit the earth.

As the preacher stood there, the television came blaring to life. He ran to turn down the volume so he could make sense out of what was happening. A newscaster was crying—yes, crying.

Scientists are fairly certain that they have finally determined exactly what has happened."

The newsman tried to continue, but the scenes being broadcast were too terrible for words to describe. The network left him sobbing on a lonely south Florida beach while a stunned anchorman tried to continue from the studio.

It seems the big storm that blew over Florida last week carried with it an airborne AIDS virus that we suspected existed, but never really saw. The swamps of south Florida apparently acted as incubator for the virus, which grew faster than anyone suspected was possible."

The virus incubated in the swamp and mutated into a form that seems to render it fatal with only one incidental contact with the lungs. Death is reported to appear almost painless, and nearly instantaneous."

Nevertheless, death is death, no matter how painless or instant.

Yesterday's storm blew the virus north and west in the counter-clockwise movement of air typical in a low pressure system. Nearly half the population of Florida has succumbed to the virus. Scientists estimate that 98 percent of the population will be dead by nightfall."

The preacher stood in silence as the reports continued to come in. He hardly twinged at the pictures from the Orlando area, where an estimated 40,000 people—men, women, and mostly children—died in less than one hour.

Not even the sight of army blockades trying to keep the people from fleeing northward, away from the death that crept steadily and relentlessly over the land, made much of an impression. Nor did it seem to bother him that the weather satellite tracked the path of the storm, with its deadly judgement, deep into the heart of America.

They deserve it!"

He scowled as he turned off the TV, only to have it turn on again of its own accord.

Reluctantly the preacher watched as the television, with an apparent mind of its own, moved from channel to channel. Scenes of horror and suffering appeared on each station. In Atlanta a stadium full of sports fans lay forever silent.

In Memphis a shopping mall became an unwilling sepulcher for hundreds of afternoon shoppers.

In major airports all along the southeastern coast the burning wreckage of hundreds of airliners were smoking testimonies to the merciless carnage. Reports of hundreds of pilots searching frantically for a safe place to land—a place that was both free from the virus and close enough to be reached before they ran out of fuel—filled the airways. Highways also were littered with twisted wreckage as black and angry smoke rolled furiously skyward, marking each spot where yet more victims had met The Judgement.

The television continued its slow, almost monotonous scroll of stations. Some were off the air; others were running old movies as though oblivious to the carnage outside. One station was apparently abandoned, except for two anchormen slumped over their desks, victims of The Judgement. A lone TV camera stood skewed to one side with no operator.

In a surge of triumphant self-righteousness, the preacher again turned off the TV. Once again, it came on of its own accord. He then angrily grabbed the cord of the television, ripped it from the wall, and

Yanked the other end of the cord victoriously from the back of the set.

For a moment he stood there in silence, but before he could feel any relief, the television once again came blaring to life.

"It's as though it's Judgement Day,"
a nameless voice spoke with chilling finality.

"Government officials continue to tell us that the plague is contained, but these pictures from around the country tell a much different story. These images are live from Washington, D.C."

The pictures moved from city to city as the announcer detailed the carnage like a sportscaster announces the evening basketball scores.

"Philadelphia, Newark, Providence, Hartford, Boston, Bangor..."

The shroud of death rolled without mercy up the eastern seaboard, killing everything in its path.

"California always gets off!"

the preacher shouted with helpless frustration.

"I just can't understand it! If anyone deserves The Judgement, Californians do."

He pounded the top of the television with both fists in anger.

Suddenly the screen went blank, only to have it reappear moments later with the sound of his own voice gleefully pronouncing The Judgement.

"If anyone sees this man, please call your local police. He is wanted for questioning concerning the virus. Some FBI agents have confirmed that a new hypothesis is emerging concerning this deadly virus. Health officials are now saying that there is absolutely no way this virus could have established its deadly course of its own accord. They are speculating that it is a possible act of terrorism by a fringe religious group based somewhere on the East Coast."

One more the TV abruptly scrolled to another station.

"What was that?"

The man of God instantly felt cold and clammy, and his breathing became more rushed. Suddenly, he felt very alone.

Could they really think that I might have had something to do with this?

He thought to himself. But he brushed it off with a nervous laugh that didn't really give him any peace.

Meanwhile, the TV blared on from another terror-stricken city as yet another newscaster continued the almost monotonous review of the macabre terror that was now nationwide.

"Airport quarantine efforts seem to have failed. All planes and passengers from the East Coast are being held in hangars for fear of The Judgement. Hundreds have already died there."

The TV moved mercilessly to another station.

"Here in L.A., government officials now speculate that a radical fringe religious element has indeed orchestrated this virus release from the Caribbean."

The preacher pounded the television. Another announcer continued,

"Reports coming in from all over the city indicate that this airborne virus was indeed carried to the West Coast and released in the air. Health officials are convinced that it is part of a conspiracy devised by a small religious organization that some say may be a cult. Officials say they need to find the leader to get the antidote.

"If anyone sees this man,"

the preacher was appalled to see his own picture flashed on nationwide television,

"please contact local officials. You should consider him armed and very dangerous."

Unparalleled fear now gripped the preacher. With a quick move of desperation, he lifted the TV from its stand and threw it out the fifth-story window, shattering the glass as it fell toward the ground.

He ran to the window and watched it hit the ground and explode with unearthly explosion that rose back up to the window and threw him against the wall.

Suddenly the angel appeared before him. Through blurry eyes of semiconsciousness, the preacher saw the angel's look of deep regret and pity.

"What are you so upset about?"
the oracle of God indignantly asked the angel.

"You've got it all wrong. They were after me. I am not the enemy! I am on God's side, remember? I am the one pronouncing The Judgement."

The angel stood in silence. There was not much that could be said. Our preacher just did not get it. I guess the angel knew that if he gave the preacher enough rope, he just might...well, let's just say it's best not to engage your mouth when your heart is not connected to your brain.

Then the angel finally spoke.

"You are not going to make this easy, are you? Just remember, it could have been much easier."

"Just what does that mean?" the preacher asked angrily.

But the angel was through speaking. He was not one to argue. Besides, the next event would speak quite plainly to our righteous man of God. With one final look of pity, the angel clapped his hands and disappeared in a splash of blinding light.

"I wonder what that was all about,"

the preacher huffed as he crawled into bed. "At least that's all over."

The angel was right. The preacher had no idea. To the preacher, it seemed he had barely closed his eyes when he was rocked by explosion that threw him far from the comfort of his hotel room, right into the center of The Judgement he himself had contrived and orchestrated. There would be no one to blame for this one. He had told the angel he knew better. He was sure that The Judgement was the only way. Now he would experience it firsthand.

The Angel and the Judgment
by Don Nori
ISBN 1-56043-154-7